MEMOIRS FROM THE POTTER'S WHEEL

© 2009 by Katrina Fox

ISBN-13: 978-0-615-41454-6
ISBN-10: 0-615-41454-0

Published by LuLu®
www.Lulu.com

All rights reserved. No part of this publication may be reproduced, stored in a retrieval system, or transmitted in any form or by any means- for example, electronic, photocopy, recording without the prior written permission of the publisher. The only exception is brief quotations in printed reviews.

All scripture is taken from the King James Version of the Bible, unless otherwise noted.

MEMOIRS FROM THE POTTER'S WHEEL

Katrina Fox

TABLE OF CONTENTS

INTRODUCTION

CHAPTER 1	"Why Hast Thou Made Me Thus?"
CHAPTER 2	"Vessel of Honor"
CHAPTER 3	"What's Love Got To Do With It?"
CHAPTER 4	"Life, The Jigsaw Puzzle"
CHAPTER 5	"The Dreamer"
CHAPTER 6	"Help Wanted"
CHAPTER 7	"It's A Thin Line"

CHAPTER 8	"Saved, Single & Unsatisfied"
CHAPTER 9	"That's What Friends Are For"
CHAPTER 10	"I'm A Warrior, Saturate Me"
CHAPTER 11	"Crossroads"
CHAPTER 12	"Help There's 2 Of Us"
CHAPTER 13	"You Play Too Much"

CHAPTER 14   "If It Was A Gift, Don't Throw It Away"

CHAPTER 15   "The Conclusion Of The Matter"

ACKNOWLEDGEMENTS

INTRODUCTION

The scriptures allow us to accompany Jeremiah as he journeys to a place called the Potter's House. The prophet arrives there to behold the Potter at work on His masterpiece. Although the vessel was marred in the hands of the Potter, He lovingly makes it into another vessel, "as it pleases Him", the writer accounts. The Lord then ends Jeremiah's vision by making a plea to Israel, His chosen people and asking, "Can I not do with you as this Potter has done?" I find it amazing that although Jeremiah's vision was seen thousands of years ago, our Heavenly Father, the Supreme Potter and Master Builder, still makes the same plea to His children today.

The challenge for the Potter is the same as it was in that day. We have become so hard hearted and regimented in our own ways. Our individual agendas for our lives simply prohibit us from being the moldable piece of clay that the Potter so desperately needs us to be. Without our flexibility, it is virtually impossible for His plan to be fulfilled in our lives. However, In spite of ourselves, God is still so good to us. That's why I thank Him for His grace and His mercy. I thank Him for how He has kept me as He lovingly and patiently shaped my life on His wheel.

I say "thank you" to the Potter for being so gracious with this stubborn, disobedient lump of clay. And thank you for the vessels that you used along the path of my journey to complete Your plans for me. I can never thank you enough Jesus for the holy men and women of God that sacrificed their time and gave of themselves for my personal deliverance when I was a teenager. They were willing to be of service for the mentoring of my future. A future that I was not even cognizant of. They could have sat back content with their knowledge of Christ, and never shared with me the intensity of His love for me, and His passion for using me in this specific moment in time. Through their love for the Lord, coupled with their love and concern for dying souls, they were relentless in prayer and the teaching of God's Word. Committed and determined to bring me, along with so many others, to the knowledge of Jesus Christ. They have passed the baton of fervor to my heart to carry the Gospel in a way that reaches beyond the conventional judgmental message of the past.

Through each course of my journey, with every tossing wind and tumultuous wave of trouble, Jesus was there. He has at times used various people, places, and situations as the catalysts to lovingly bring my focus back to Him and to His call on my life. Every situation, although overwhelming at the time, was used by the Potter to work out the "kinks" in my armor and to burn out any traces of impurities. I did not always know this was His means of process, but I can now boldly proclaim that what the devil meant for evil, God turned it around for my good. In spite of everything that my enemy attempted to do to make sure that the odds were stacked against me, I managed by the grace of God to still emerge the victor! For it is Jesus who ultimately and consistently grants to us the victory. Thank God for relinquishing to us so much love through the gift of salvation. It is in fact the key to life and without it, life holds no real sense of hope or purpose.

Never allow yourself to be manipulated into the boxes that man has designed for you. Remembering as the scriptures admonish "whatever your hands find to do, do it with all your might, as unto the Lord and not unto man; knowing that it is from the Lord that you will receive the reward." Everyone's vocation or call is not the same, but the commitment, zeal and focus should always be the same....**Intense**. We must understand our mission and be willing to accept it even as we uncontrollably reel at times on the wheel of the Potter. It is key that you never, ever read the headlines that people have written about you…for reading them will only discourage you. Do what God has assigned to your hands, knowing that the battle is not yours, but the Lord's. For God is not unrighteous to forget your work and labor of love that you have showed toward His name. Man may forget, but God never forgets, and it is He that has promised to pay every man according as his work shall be.

So please join me as I relive **my** journey down to the Potter's House. For my prayer is that as I diary my dialogues and memories of the Master's reworking of this lump of clay, that you, my fellow lumps of clay, will begin to understand your experiences and the highs and lows of being in the hands of the Potter. It is with exuberance of heart from one lump of clay to another, that I greet you in the name that is above every name. I introduce to you my Keeper, my Provider, my Friend, my Coach, my Confidant, my Lord, my Potter…Jesus Christ the Righteous.

CHAPTER I

WHY HAST THOU MADE ME THUS?

I remember being a young babe in Christ and relishing in the wonder of the Potter's Wheel. What a wonderful analogy the writer uses to describe my relationship with the Father. I pondered the Potter, coupled with the time and the intricacies invested as He studied each piece of clay. I loved to think about how the Father first had to imagine what He wanted me to be like. There were questions He must have asked Himself, and then decisions He made based upon how I would be displayed in time. Isn't it amazing to note that every touch of His hand and every indentation of His chisel has been specifically designed by Him for me?

"What type of heart should she have?" He asked himself. "Should it be one that only loves when loved in return? Or should it be a heart like My Son's heart that would cause her to give all she had for a lost and cruel world? Hearts like those are easily broken," He replied to himself. So what shall I do to this lump of clay that would ensure her refusal to retaliate every time this heart is broken? It must be able to mend quickly and return to love again, only stronger the next time. I will seal it with Agape; it is the most potent fruit in my garden. Unconditional love…a love so rich that would cause a man to lay down his life for his friend." The same friendship that Jesus had, the kind of love that says, I'll take your place. Oh what a blessing to be the friend of God.

Many times in life we don't understand our friends. The decisions they make, the paths they choose. Nevertheless, we remain their friend…we love them still. The true friend relationship with the Father works the same way. We don't always like the molding and the shaping of the Potter's hands, the twisting and pulling of the clay as He rids it of its mars and defects. We say that we want to be used of God and without spot or wrinkle, but how much do we really mean that once we begin to feel the fury of the Potter's wheel? I penned many of these memoirs while spinning uncontrollably on that same wheel. Therefore, it has been my experience that this wheel is not a place that we often volunteer to go because of the discomfort associated with it.

Did you know that when a Potter is molding his masterpiece, there are times when he will add coarse, grainy matter in varying quantities to the clay in order to achieve a particular effect? A certain amount of coarse grain helps the vessel to retain its shape in firing. The Lord teaches us through His word that each one of us must experience our own version of the fiery furnace, just as the three Hebrew boys did. It is then actually His concern for us that allows Him to grant permission to the devil to throw some dirt into the game. It's so that we won't fall apart when we go through the fire. And every vessel, or precious metal that would be a vessel of value, must be exposed to intense heat. There is no getting around it. No shortcuts, Hallelujah! Unless you just want to be a cheap copy. So the Potter, who in His wisdom, we now understand adds sand, fine stones, and ground shells, to His lump of clay. He does these things only because they will assist in the preparation of the clay before kneading it into workable condition. The clay could have become hardened, inflexible and not pliable due to its past experience. In other words, unwilling to be molded. Oh, but the Potter has a way with His clay, for He is a Master at what He does, and He's had this planned since the beginning of time.

A dear friend of my Pastor's once informed us during a sermon he preached that the Father had to work on the "ugly" areas in our lives so that He could work it **up**, and then He would work it **out**. Because of this working up and out, the Potter will do what may seem cruel to the lump of clay. By flattening it, and then shaping by pressing it against the inside or outside of a mold. The ball of clay may also be pinched into the desired shape. And you wondered why so often you felt pressed, and pulled, and pinched beyond measure.

The Potter's wheel, invented in the 4th millennium B.C., is a flat disk that rotates horizontally on a pivot. Using this method, the Potter is able to use both his hands, placing one on the inside of the clay, and the other on the outside of the clay. This procedure provided the Potter's hands the necessary freedom that enabled him to shape the ball of clay upward into a pot from its original form. The most sophisticated Pottery making technique is called Wheel Throwing. That same lump of clay which had been thrown, and centered on the rotating wheel, was now at the mercy of the unrestricted creativity of the Potter's hands. Do you still wonder why you felt as though your life was spinning out of control at times? Now you know- it is because it really was! The consolation is that the Potter has you on His wheel, you didn't just happen to fall into the situation that you're in. You are placed on the wheel by divine assignment, and you are exactly where the Potter needs you to be.

I know the songwriter made it sound pretty when she spoke of the Potter's House. She sang about the love, joy and peace that was at the Potter's House, but there was no warning about what really goes on there. Let me tell you that the Potter's wheel is no joke, but it's worth the trip, I promise you that. So stay right there. Don't you dare jump off that wheel! I know it hurts, I know it gets rough, I know you feel like you're going in circles, but the Father wants to present you faultless before the presence of His Glory. He wants to display His glory through you right now, not just when you get to Heaven. Stay right there and let Him mold you into what He desires for you to be, for the Potter is working His personal labor of love. And when He finally unveils you, you'll be just the treasure for which an unfulfilled world has been looking.

CHAPTER II
VESSEL OF HONOR

Has the Word of God not forewarned us that every man's work shall be tried by fire to see what sort it is? There is so much that is done to the clay as it rotates seemingly out of control, only to then be thrust into an open fire at temperatures of 1202-1382 degrees Fahrenheit. It is interesting to note though, that before the Potter subjects his clay to the fire; he allows it to air dry so that it won't break during the firing process. Thank God that He gives us a moment to breathe. In His wisdom, He realizes that a broken vessel can carry no water. It can offer no refreshment and cannot adequately display its full beauty. Our God knows our frame and how much we can bear. He recognizes that we are only clay, mere dust, so He will always with our temptation make a way of escape that we may be able to bear it.

Remember however, that it is only sophisticated Pottery that has the distinction of going into the firing oven. These containers which are capable of providing both refreshment to the body, and/or pleasure to the eye, qualify for the unique category known as Vessel of Honor.

Becoming a vessel of honor is in fact a matter of choice. You must choose to go through the entire process. It is no easy task. Remember that the worth of a metal is determined by how much heat it can take. There are various types of metal such as iron, steel and silver. But then there are those types that are known as precious metals such as gold and platinum. Would you rather be valued as silver or platinum? When the scriptures speak of the many vessels in the house of God, some to honor and some to dishonor, it speaks of the part that we play in determining which we will be. Every man can be a vessel of honor he admonishes, if he first purges himself. He is instructing us that in order to be a vessel of honor, one prepared and meet for the Master's use, we cannot be made of common, every day materials. We cannot build with wood, stubble or hay and become a vessel of honor. All these would be burned up immediately beyond recognition and unable to withstand the heat of the furnace. In addition, common items like wood, stubble and hay would require no extra effort beyond the norm to obtain, for they can be found at your local feed and seed store. You don't have to go **down** to acquire them. Yes, they too serve some purpose, but they hold no particular attraction and no lasting value because they can be found anywhere. They are **ordinary**, not honorable, and always remember that ordinary is your enemy. Ahh, but the extraordinary, that which is valuable and weighty in the Kingdom, understands the need for fire. Just like a fine piece of gold, silver, or yes even that very sophisticated piece of Pottery, high levels of heat are required to rid impurities that would decrease their value.

In this walk, the choice really is ours. Paul speaks of his desire to know the Lord, but not just to know Him in the power of His resurrection, but also to know Him in the fellowship of His suffering. We love the power of His resurrection part; it is the fellowship of His suffering that we have a problem with. You see, we don't get to know the Jesus that Isaiah describes as despised and rejected of men, a man of sorrows and well acquainted with grief. That's not the part of being like Jesus that we particularly want to experience. That is why I reiterate that being a vessel of honor is indeed a decision, not inevitable.

Merriam-Webster defines the word acquaint in this way...to cause to know **personally**. This is not a distant or casual affair that Jesus has with grief, they are bedfellows, "road dogs" if you will.

But I submit to you that this isn't what we're talking about when we pray those wonderful prayers to the Father of how we long to know Jesus and be like Jesus. We are talking about the Jesus that walked on the water, and the Jesus who made blind eyes to see, the Jesus that cast out devils and was a threat to the religious order of His day. That's the Jesus we want to be, the glamorous Jesus. The reality of the matter is that to be like Jesus, there will be many days that your heart will hurt so badly, you will think it is about to burst out of your chest. To be like Jesus, you'll find that after you have worn yourself out, being there for everybody else's problems, you won't be able to find one friend that can help you to get through your own. You will find that you will experience Gethsemane time and time again. And what's at Gethsemane? Loneliness is at Gethsemane, despair is at Gethsemane, abandonment, confusion and doubt are at Gethsemane…yes lots of doubt. "I know what I said Father, but can you find another way?...this hurts too much!" There is a below the belt punch that comes just when you think that you can't hurt anymore. Only the Word of God and the Holy Ghost can sustain you at those times. Yes, the Holy Ghost…He is a mighty keeper and trusty insulator. What does insulation in a house do? It seals what's on the inside of that house whether that be cool air in the summer time or warm air in the winter. There is a thermostat placed on the inside of the house which will adjust what is on the inside to compensate for what's trying to infiltrate from the outside. Yes, the sweet Holy Spirit who keeps all the fire and energy that you need safely protected on the inside of you, while making sure that none of the impurities from outside infiltrate your desire to do God's will. The Holy Ghost is a resuscitator! Just when the enemy thinks you're down for the count, grace and mercy will come and revive your soul again. No wonder David said when my heart is overwhelmed; lead me to the Rock that is higher than I. God knows how to deliver you, heal you, renew you and then reveal to you why you had to endure what you've endured in order to become who you are…a vessel of honor. Do not be deceived by an already defeated foe. He thinks that by using a series of events and people that he can change your destiny. The Potter is the only legitimate Author and Finisher of your faith. He's already written the script for your life, all you have to do is follow His lead. Allow Him to be the writer, producer and director of this awesome coming attraction...your life...your destiny....your unveiling. This same Potter is also your "Wonderful Counselor" as Isaiah calls Him. A counselor has the power to resolve, to set at peace or rest. That is why your communication with Him is so vital. Notice that you never come away from a conversation with the Lord feeling confused, depressed or frustrated. It is only when we attempt to do things on our own, apart from asking what He wants, that we experience the negativity. Communion with the Potter as He molds you, will make your transition from Egypt to your promise land much smoother.

The writer Jeremiah is careful to point out that he went **down** to the Potter's House. So you have to go down first. There can be no resurrection without a burial, so remember Jesus is your perfect example. Down hurts, down gets ugly, down gets frustrating and down gets weary. But down also gets you all power, down is where you get your character, down is where you get your fortitude, down is where you really get to know the Lily of the Valley at His best. The scriptures plainly tell us that there can be no ascension until there is a descent. So down is where you go to find priceless pearls, and down is where you go to drill for pure crude oil. Yes! Down is where you mine for diamonds, gold and precious metals. I thank God for going down, for it is only after I have suffered with Him, that I am able to then reign with Him.

Know this my fellow lumps of clay, that no matter how much we squirm, beg, plead or cry, the Omniscient Potter will not remove you from the oven until He knows that you are ready. And how can He tell when you're done? He can tell you are done, when nothing matters any more. He knows that you're done when you can serve the Lord with some pep in your step, even when it seems as though He's not granting you the desires of your heart. You're done when you're so addicted to the relationship that you have with him, that you can't wait to get somewhere quiet and alone just to make love to Him. When I speak of making love to the Lord, I speak figuratively of course and not in the physical sense. Although as in the natural, it is a time for you to set aside for Him. Not to ask Him for anything, just to thank Him for everything. To weep if you need to without embarrassment, and to enjoy the opportunity to block out the entire world for a time of passionate communication with Him. You're done when everybody you have ever counted on and leaned upon, has failed you. You're done when in spite of all these things you can let the devil know to his face that he can't take anything away from you because you don't have anything. And that he can't give you anything because you already have everything! The songwriter said "I'm yours Lord! Everything I am, and everything I'm not. I'm yours Lord, try me now and see. See if I can be completely yours". When you give yourself to someone in this way, whatever they do with you is okay. Their loving makes everything around you more tolerable. You feel full and complete, entire and wanting nothing. I'm yours Jesus, tears on my pillow…..**yours.** Knives in my back…**still yours**! Husband walked off and left me….**yours Lord**….children flunking in school…**still yours Lord**. The doctor says there's nothing more he can do…**yours Lord**! Laid off from my job….**still yours Lord**! Why? Because I remember that every time the "fire" gets turned up, it only pushes me closer to the destiny that the Potter has so lovingly and specifically designed for me. I am then reminded also that it takes His grace to sustain me and mold this lump of clay. Every crack in this vessel tells of the mistakes that I've made, but it also serves as a reminder to me that the Potter, who loves me so much, will take the time to fix every crack and remove every blemish until nothing is left to see but His fingerprints.

CHAPTER III

WHAT'S LOVE GOT TO DO WITH IT?

I think it is safe to assume that all those who peruse the pages of this journey of mine, have at one time or another been "in love"....or at least thought that they were. What I've learned from life's experiences, but mostly from the love of God, is that love is authenticated not only when it is felt, but when it is lived. Over the past 41 years I've had many people tell me how much they love me. However good their intentions, they were not always able to live up to the extent of that statement.

LOVE...a very small word that carries a great impact in every human being's life. The very connotation of the word carries the ability to cross barriers of race, creed, gender, religious persuasion, language, time, and distance. Have you ever noticed how different you are when you are in love? There is a glow about you that people can plainly see. Just the mention of your beloved's name can bring a smile to your face. One thought of that special someone can have such an effect on you, that it has the ability to change the course of an entire day. There is an ache that approaches at some point during the day, as you long for the presence and touch of one who brings solace and refuge to your world. It matters not how many other people may be with you, if the one who fills your heart is absent.

I can remember being so immersed in longing for the one that I loved, that I would call just because I wanted to hear his voice. Nothing in particular that I needed to say or hear, I just wanted to be reminded of what his voice sounded like. Can we honestly say that we feel the same about the voice of our blessed Savior? Does our day just seem incomplete without some connection to His presence? The touch of His hand, His warm embrace and His still small voice? Do we long for these sensations from Him the way that we do from other humans? Or are we content to go from church service to church service, only talking to Him when we need some sort of "fix", never spending the intimate time alone that it takes to fall completely in love with Him, and build a formidable and lasting relationship.

In prayer one day, I heard the Lord say to me "by yourself". I remember saying okay Lord, you want me to get by myself? I was already contemplating making a very critical

"Abraham move" where I would be leaving my family, friends, church and all that had become familiar to me over the last 12 years. I had already come to a place in my life where I knew that I was at the threshing floor of life, and that the Lover of my soul was about to do some separating. I was finally okay with the thought of knowing that certain people I loved could not go with me to this next level. I remembered learning about Ruth and Boaz and how Ruth met her Kinsman Redeemer at the threshing floor from one of Pastor Carpenter's sermons. My mind rushed back to how in the book of Ruth, Naomi had instructed Ruth to wash herself. Metaphorically she was telling Ruth to wash away the residue of her past so that she could step into the destiny that God had prepared for her. I tearfully said "yes Lord" as I humbled myself to accept once again what I felt the Potter was asking of me.

However, as I kept listening for His instruction, I realized that the Lord was talking about more than me just getting by myself. As I pondered the words "by yourself" he asked me, "What does the word by mean?" I immediately found a dictionary and scurried to find what else the Lord was trying to reveal to me. To my surprise, I discovered that the Lord was not just telling me to separate from people physically. The definition of the word by is next to or beside. He wanted me to get next to myself. He wanted me to better learn about myself, because in doing so I would inevitably find it easier to be more open with him. Just like in human relationships, it is very often in our spiritual walk that we hide ourselves from ourselves. We are self deceived, and love to make excuses for ourselves, while we blame others for the situations that we find ourselves in. Coming to grips with one's self and discovering what motivates you and makes you tick is very empowering. It opens up the flood gates to unfolding what your true purpose in life is. You begin to very clearly recognize what you do not want, which can be just as powerful and knowing what you do want.

This "by myself" time has allowed me to understand why it has been so hard for me to trust God for a happy ending. Why it has been so difficult to truly receive the words of Jeremiah 29:11 where he says "I know my plans for you, to prosper you and not to harm you. Plans to give you hope and a future". It is difficult to trust someone that has hurt you. It takes a release of control in allowing yourself to be vulnerable enough to possibly be hurt by this person again. And who wants to volunteer to be hurt again? Well, you do if you want to be crucified, you do if you want to be raised in power with Him, and you do if you want to begin healing.

Can you imagine Jesus kicking and screaming on His way to the cross? What a mess that would have been. He had to **voluntarily** give His life, not have it taken, if He was to be the sweet smelling sacrifice and appeasement to God that we needed Him to be. With all the power that resided inside of Him, He chose to be **led** as a lamb to the slaughter, not forced, so that He could be the acceptable propitiation for our sins. No crucifixion, no resurrection. He **chose** to endure the cross and despise the shame. Why? Not just because of love for us, but because He saw the joy that was set before Him, as Paul so eloquently describes, not just the current pain of His circumstance. By the time that Jesus made it to Calvary, the devil couldn't touch Him. See, He wasn't going to Calvary unprepared, that's where Gethsemane came in. Jesus had already died in the garden when He said "nevertheless, not My will, but thine." The Garden of Gethsemane was Jesus' preparation for His cross. Jesus realized that you can't win a prize if you refuse to run the race. And you certainly cannot run the race if you refuse to prepare. Even knowing all of this, having Jesus as our perfect example, we still choose to avoid our crosses. Then we want to ask questions like "Lord, how could you let this happen?" or "Lord, why **would** you let this happen?" Many of us would never admit it, but we are secretly angry with the Potter for the things that He has allowed to happen to us. We harbor mistrust for what He will do with our future if we completely yield to Him. At various times in our lives, we take the reigns, believing that we can do a better job at charting our course than God. We carry on a casual acquaintance with Him, instead of the intense and passionate love fest that He desires to have with us, because it is safe. You can't hurt me if I don't give myself to you wholly and completely, if I don't make myself vulnerable to you. So His voice becomes a burden to us instead of the sweet sound of the one we love, which should be music to our ears. And all because we fear that He will ask us to do something that is painful or uncomfortable to our flesh and our will. Bishop Smith would often remind us in his messages that "if we were still hurting, it was only because we hadn't died yet". As soon as you stop fighting and being upset that you are even on the cross, just give up and die, God can get the glory from your resurrection. Remember, a dead man feels nothing.

You can kick him, spit on him, even talk about his Momma and you'll get no reaction from him, because he is dead.

I learned that sometimes the Potter has to hurt you to heal you. Remember His conversation with the disciples in John Chapter 15? He tells them in a parable what it is like to love Him and remain in Him. He explains that He is the True Vine, His Father is the husbandman, and we are the branches. As such, His Father will purge every branch that does bear fruit, in order that it will bring forth more fruit. Purge…hmmm doesn't that mean to cut? Okay last time I checked, cutting, in any sense of the word, will bring pain or discomfort to that which is being cut. But something it also brings besides the pain and discomfort, is change to that which is being cut. If you will just chew on that concept for a moment, and let it digest, my goodness, how it will bless you. Anyhow, Jesus goes on to say that outside of the Vine, the branches can do nothing, so that they must remain with Him. For in doing so, they will be able to bear more fruit, and have the benefit of asking whatsoever they will, and it being done. So in plain terms, He advises us that He **is** going to cut us, but He needs us to stick with Him while He does the cutting. If we stick with Him, and don't avoid the cutting, we can get anything we need out of

Him by simply asking for it. Powerful isn't it? Yes it is, but you can't be a casual acquaintance and get that kind of benefit. You have to be willing to get cut, hurt, and then die. Too much to ask of some of us. I realize that, but that is why we stay in the stagnant places of our existence that we so often do.

For example, I watched my mother, who was going through so much pain with genetic arthritis. Her knees had gotten to the place where the cartilage was completely gone, causing her a great deal of discomfort. The absence of cartilage meant that as she walked, bone simply hit against bone minus any type of cushion. Well, she finally decided to have the knee replaced based on the advice of her physician, who told her that the pain she felt would only continue to worsen without the surgery. After surgery, it seemed my mother was hurting much more than before the surgery. We all began to wonder if this had been the right thing to do. As I listened to her on one of my visits to the hospital, she explained to me how excruciating her recovery was. The pain of therapy was almost more than she could bear, as she had to relearn to do the simplest of tasks on her own. I watched the grimace on her face as the new knee reminded her that it was there, and I told her

"Mommy, I know it's difficult right now, but the doctor had to hurt you in order to heal you." I reminded her that if she could just hold on and make it through the recovery, the pain would be a distant memory once she was completely healed. Her faith as she praised God through every hurting day was a reminder to me to allow the Potter to do with me what He needed to in order to purge away all the dross from my life. Knowing that when He was done, I would not only be whole, complete and healed, but I would be ready for service. Voluntarily saying yes to "being cut" or pruning is never an easy task, but it is a profitable one nonetheless. Jesus tells us that every fruitful or profitable branch understands and accepts this. We need His help to even desire His pruning shears. My choir would sing a song that says "God wants a yes." Many times I've had to beg that same God for the ability to even say yes. I knew that He wanted a yes, but just the thought of the pain that yes would bring, inspired me all the more to say No! I know I'm not alone in that sentiment. If we could only convince ourselves to stick with His voice though, and obey His command, we would without fail become better mothers, wives, teachers, sisters, friends and disciples as we endure the pruning. Sometimes His voice will lead us into a wilderness, but remember that once Jesus exited the temptation of the wilderness, the bible says He returned in the power of the spirit. The power didn't come before the wilderness, it came afterwards!

I can remember as a young girl, I would play a song on my organ that said "I come to the garden alone, while the dew is still on the roses. And the voice I hear falling on my ear, the Son of God discloses. And He walks with me and He talks with me and He tells me I am his own. And the joy we share, as we tarry there....none other has ever known." This song is such a sweet reminder of how precious time alone making love to Jesus can be. What I mean here is that the alone time spent in prayer and meditation with the Lord can be viewed as an analogy to the natural connection shared between two that share physical intimacy. You can discover a lot about a person during a lovemaking session. That alone time with each other brings about vulnerability and trust that is uncommon with any other type of relationship. Nothing can make you feel more at someone's mercy, than being naked and allowing another person to do with you as they please. Can you imagine the impact we could have on this world if we just allowed the Potter the pleasure of that even twice a week? Nothing between you & Him, nothing hidden, nothing to be ashamed of, just a time that you and the Lord share talking about the things that you desire, need, or even sometimes fear. Your time to tell Him how much you need Him, love Him and can't live without Him. Your time to thank Him for His guidance, favor and grace.

Isn't it amazing how lightly we take falling in love with Jesus? We tend to fall in love with other human beings much more intensely and easily than we fall in love with the Lord, the one that has done so much for us. Greater love hath no man than this, Jesus once said, that a man would lay down His life for His friend. Yet, it is a love that we all too often have taken for granted. There have been times when I have picked up the phone just to say "I love you." How about you? I knew that there would also be the reassuring response of "I love you too" in reply. This always did something for my psyche, not just when I was having a good day, but particularly if I was having a bad day.

I had to examine my relationship with the Lord and realize that it becomes so easy to have other gods before Him. It becomes second nature to love Him nonchalantly, while we pour it on thick, and love others without inhibition. Do people know how much in love you are with God? I'm not talking about bibles always shoved up to your nose, or bumper stickers, scarves and bracelets that say "I love Jesus." No, I speak of a genuine "glow" that says to everyone you come in contact with, I have something that not everyone is privileged to have. Everyone is not fortunate enough to find their true love. Those of us who have, take true pride in showing others what being in love looks like. When you're in love, you have a tendency to show it off to others. The pictures of your significant other are displayed upon your desk at work even now. You are proud whenever someone asks "And who might *this* be?" Remember on Valentine's Day when that huge bouquet of roses arrived at your desk? How proud you were when a co-worker said, "Wow, somebody must really love you!" There was a warm sensation which seemed physical, but is clearly emotional, that brought comfort inside when you were reassured of how much you were loved and appreciated. So tell me, how many times did you go out of your way today to let the lover of your soul know how much you love and appreciate Him? How many times did you call Him up just to say "I love you?"

What's love got to do with it, I ask you my fellow lumps of clay? May I venture to say EVERYTHING? Love changes your world, even when nothing in your world has changed. The book of Corinthians describes a love to us that is so unique, understood in its depth only by those who are true lovers of God. Paul takes the time to describe love to us in the truest sense of the word. The type of love that is unconditional and is consistently given without hesitation, even at those times when reciprocity is absent. The person who truly falls in love with you does so free of conditions. They do not try to change you, but somehow change comes inevitably as a result of their love. I can remember being very bitter, apprehensive to trust or believe that true love was even possible in life. Sometimes the disappointments of the past can leave very deep scars. It will cause you to be robbed of your belief system in a God who is good and faithful and has reserved only the best for you. The word of God declares that true love casts out fear, and true love keeps no account of wrong doing.

Love has the most powerful eraser known to man, one that is capable of removing all doubt, fear, and apprehension, then subsequently replacing those past emotions with undaunting faith. Love will cause you to accept what you thought you never would, live where you don't want to live, sacrifice what you previously didn't dream of sacrificing and give when you thought you had nothing left to give. True love has the power to make you laugh when you should be crying and stand when you should be running. I know a love that enables you to face every battle you thought you couldn't face. For the essence of true love will provide courage that one never even knew they possessed. This is the love that I'm privileged to partake of. This is the love that I've come to know by falling completely for this man called Jesus. He has been my friend through it all. Not once has He turned His back on me, or changed His mind about me. His faithfulness has remained intact, even when I was not His faithful bride. I've got it bad for Him and I don't care who knows it. Why should I care? He had it bad for me first! And that deep "love Jones" for me accompanied Him throughout His journey here on earth. It wooed Him all the way to Gethsemane and beyond to Calvary. What does love have to do with it? Everything! For His love is my life.

CHAPTER IV

LIFE, THE JIGSAW PUZZLE

When relationship is addressed properly, you can truly understand that not only is relationship the sacrifice of one's self, but there is also agreement to accept others just as they are. Sometimes you must approach the unapproachable by breaking down the barriers that keep both you and the other person's desire to be loved in confinement. Relationship means that in one way or another, you leave pieces of yourself with each and every person that you have ever loved. Pieces that you can never get back again, yes many broken pieces. Although the sound of that seems disheartening at first, I now realize in retrospect that pieces are not such a terrible aftermath when you are dealing with a Potter who is the Master of broken pieces.

Just like a puzzle, you have to visualize what you want the finished product to look like. All the little pieces, once put together in the way that the original creator intended, will produce upon completion not only something that is pleasant to look at, but that which is gratifying to the one who was responsible for completion, as well. It does not matter whether the puzzle was a 100-piece project or a 1,000-piece project; the feeling of accomplishment is the same. In the beginning it can be discouraging when you look at the fact that you have a thousand discombobulated pieces and no earthly idea of where to begin, based on what the beautiful picture on the box is showing you. The picture portrayed on the front is complete and does not tell the story of the frustration experienced in piecing it all together. Initially, you think "this is going to be impossible or it will take me forever to figure this thing out". But if you can only convince yourself to make a start, you'll find that as you go along, the puzzle ceases to look like 1,000 discombobulated pieces, and starts to take on the form of something recognizable.

Life, the jigsaw puzzle is really the same. Life itself, is completely about purpose, not just process. If we focus on the process, it can be discouraging at times, and prevent the end result, which is to discover the Potter's intent for you being on this earth. Life, however, is not only about finding your purpose, but about holding onto it once you do. But what does the word purpose really mean? Before the book "Purpose Driven Life" was published, I'd pondered this question and have even preached on the subject. I found in my study, that the word purpose means what one intends or wants to accomplish, a plan, aim, result or effect. The reason for which a thing exists; determination or resolve; to be deliberate or intentional. Wow! I thought to myself "purpose is much deeper than I realized.". It enables you to use your God-given talents, gifts and abilities to fulfill a need in the world. Purpose is not only what you do, but purpose is what you are. Ask yourself this question and then answer honestly. Am I on purpose?

Why should you ask this question? Because not knowing your purpose in life makes life even more puzzling. The absence of this knowledge at times will cause not only discontentment and a feeling of hopelessness, but also feelings of disconnection and bitterness. More often than not, the circumstances of life can cast a dark cloud of gloom upon us. What I have found in my own life is that my sense of purpose has enabled me to keep pressing when everything around me said GIVE UP! I am convinced that many of the people in our society that suffer with bouts of depression and anxiety, do so because they feel worthless, void of any real sense of purpose for their lives.

People on purpose awake each morning with clarity and determination. The excitement that the Potter has placed in their heart propels them forward even when there is opposition. There is an urgency that says to all opposition, "Look, I've got somewhere to go!" Your destiny calls out to you, not allowing you to rest, as your spirit man leads you by a voice heard only by you. Your purpose can be compared to having an appointment with your hairdresser. You know that being just a few minutes late for that appointment could cause you an hour or more delay in the long run. Therefore, you allow nothing to hinder your prompt arrival for your appointed destiny in her chair. You know that the consequences of your tardiness could be substantial. Beloved, we must learn to be that aggressive and possessive regarding our spiritual appointments. Recognize that purpose is more than a goal or even an appointment. It is, in fact, a mission born in the depths of your spirit man.

The person who completes the jigsaw puzzle is actually on a mission to achieve some sense of accomplishment for a job well done. That sense of accomplishment gives purpose and meaning to the long hours, intense concentration and moments of doubt experienced. It attempts to transform the mass of confusion into a replica of the portrait displayed on the box. Your mission in life is to do the exact same thing. I've often asked the Potter to please draw my inner man and my footsteps toward the destiny that He had in mind for me when He originally thought of me. I want to be so yielded to His original plan for my life that I don't have to figure out my next move. I just have to march to the cadence of the drum beat I hear inside of my heart, His drum beat.

Therefore, I conclude that a mission is definitely what we are on. Knowing our purpose and keeping it in the forefront of our minds will guarantee that every mission impossible will become a mission accomplished. Bear in mind that when you are on purpose, you don't have to scratch, kick, fight or connive. Money, respect, love, happiness and all that you desire will come to you. There is no need to struggle and no need to squeeze yourself into situations that are either inappropriate or that you have outgrown. When you're on purpose, you don't have to squeeze in. Your place will simply open up for you. Just as the Word of God has promised, your gift will make room for you; it will simply open doors for you and bring you before great men.

The Potter has your prepared place, not man. You don't have to compete for it, nor do you have to fight to stay in it. Do not fear losing it, since you cannot be removed from it. In a puzzle, pieces don't compete because they were already created to fit where they are supposed to fit. Of course, along the way you will be challenged, but so what! Every true warrior wants and needs a challenge. A warrior feels useless unless they are somewhere defending what they believe in. The Bible says He, talking about the Potter, teaches my hands to war and my fingers to fight. A skillful warrior, however, must know when it is time to fight and when it is time to surrender for the furtherance of purpose. Jesus knew the difference. He was the epitome of power under control.

My bishop once preached a message in which he taught that there is a Judas for every Jesus. As he taught the lesson, revelation burst in my spirit. Jesus the Savior needed Judas, just in case Jesus the man changed His mind about being on purpose. Judas made sure that the humanity of Jesus in Gethsemane did not deter the purpose of Jesus the Savior at Calvary. So Judas, I have come to realize, is a part of the puzzle too. This seemingly small, but very critical insight encouraged me to hold on to my purpose by any means necessary. I needed all my Judases, just in case I changed my mind about going to the cross. They made sure I got there. I am determined now more than ever, as I face my own personal Gethsemanes and Calvarys, that I must not only take care as not to abort my purpose, but I must also not do anything that would cause a miscarriage of it either.

In infancy, both naturally and spiritually, your purpose is vague and may seem to evade you for an extended period of time. Life and its unexpected circumstances can leave you in a "funk" of disarray and confusion, while the pieces continue to look as if they will never come together. You sit on the sidelines looking at all your wrong decisions, bad moves, and constant heartaches, and wonder why you ever tricked yourself into thinking that you could accomplish such a difficult feat as this. Often we find that the plan we had pictured so perfectly in our mind does not resemble at all the shamble that our life seems to have become, just like that box full of disconnected pieces from your favorite jigsaw puzzle. Take heart my fellow lumps of clay. Stay persistent, diligent and focused on the good things that your Creator has promised. For He has said that He would not withhold any good thing from those that love Him. Therefore, with a little time, patience and perseverance, you will discover that all the pieces will one day come together. And at a time when you least expect it! That's why I insist that life is just like a jigsaw puzzle. The Potter doesn't allow you to trace His way of doing things while He's making you into what He wants you to be, and bringing you into your prepared place. You only have a faint picture of what it's supposed to look like when He's done.

So I have decided (and I hope you have too), to give Him all the pieces of your puzzle called "life." He knows what the end result is supposed to be anyway. Just yield to Him and let Him put all of the pieces in place for you. After all, He's God isn't He -- is there anything impossible with Him? The Potter does not want you to waste time trying to figure out life, the jigsaw puzzle; He only wants you to remember that you've already been figured in by the blood of Jesus Christ.

CHAPTER V
THE DREAMER

Hope deferred makes the heart sick, the wise author of Proverbs writes. How could King Solomon have known this lump of clay well enough to have penned those words thousands of years ago? How is it that he caught a glimpse of the pain that sometimes grips my heart as I experience the stagnation of my life, seemingly being held as a prisoner, while my mind dreams of and envisions all the wonder of my destined life. At times it feels like the ultimate torture. To be able to visualize and feel inside of you a destiny so real that it constantly pulls your mind towards it, yet tangibly you are seemingly never able to grasp it. A future so vivid to your spirit man, and void of anguish and struggle; yet one that your natural man can hardly see because the murkiness of your current circumstance keeps it veiled most of the time.

Is this what Joseph the dreamer felt like I ask myself. Did his heart feel the ultimate betrayal by the Potter at those dark times when the splendor of the dream that God had showed him was in constant competition with the nightmare that he was actually living? I wish that I could interview other lumps of clay. I would ask them if I was the only one who went back and forth between the love for my dream, the motivation that was fueled by that dream, and a hatred for my dream. I would ask them if they ever questioned the Potter in anger and accused Him of being nothing but a "tease" in showing them something that they never could quite apprehend. Just like Paul, I have been on a quest to apprehend that which has apprehended me. Or am I the only lump of clay that ever asked God "Why did you have to show this to me? I would be better off if you had never given me a dream." I could be like most people, satisfied with their life as it is, never having to be disappointed by dreams that don't come to fruition.

I once worked for an organization that taught us to always "sell the dream." As savvy sales agents, they instructed us in training sessions that most adults had stopped dreaming as children, but that it was our job to show them how to dream again. Working the daily grind and paying the monthly bills is all that we resolve to do in life. The majority of people I interviewed from every walk of life had stopped dreaming about the type of house they wanted to live in, the type of car they wanted to drive, and the type of vacations they wanted to take. Even further back in their minds was the type of money they wanted to have for ministry, their aging parents, and/or college savings for their children. It all now seemed so impossible, boxed into life as they had come to know it; and they all seemed to think that there was no hope for change in this late stage of the game.

But as I so often did, sitting across from those families at their kitchen tables, we must remind ourselves daily that as long as there is life, there is something to hope for. And if you dare hope for anything, surely you can train your mind to dream for those same things. Let me remind you, however, that dreams can be dangerous. Why? Because they cause you to go against the grain…to be different from most, and sometimes to be hated by those you'd least expect. You won't blend in if you're a dreamer, so if you fear being different, dreaming is not for you. My belief is that although being a dreamer may cause you to be a laughing stock, being a dreamer is also imperative. Just ask Joseph. He would tell you that he was the youngest of his brethren, and loved tremendously by his father Jacob. He was not proud or boastful, but he innocently had a dream one day and in this dream, he saw all of his brothers bow down to him in reverence. Of course it was the Potter's doing, for Joseph was minding his business, enjoying his life as it was. The excitement he felt for what God had shown him however, was not shared by his siblings. Little did he know that the joy he'd known from that glimpse of his destiny would soon be snuffed out. He had no idea that his world of contentment, peace and happiness would be turned completely upside down.

I, like Joseph, and maybe like some of you, had been going along on my merry way, minding my own business when the Potter showed me something. It was just a glimpse, but it was enough of a glimpse to give me the type of hunger that would cause me to strive every single day until I could experience what I'd seen. When the Potter gave me that "peak," my life was forever changed; A wonderful experience to say the least, seeing a life so different from my own and from any life that my family had ever known. It rejuvenated me and gave me something to think about and look forward to every day, until time set in. Time has a way of beating your dreams out of you if you allow it. Before the enemy of my life made his attempt to use time as the means of my defeat (just as he did Joseph), I would tell everyone about my dream. Family, friends, and enemies whom I thought were friends. I watched some of their pasted expressions of feigned excitement, and listened to their false encouragement while I could hear what they were really thinking inwardly. Some of them, not all.

Those that represented Joseph's siblings in my life were not my natural brethren, but my brothers and sisters in Christ. "She must be crazy! Who does she think she is anyway?" were the snide remarks that they made when I was not in their presence. And because of this, some days I was full of determination, able to believe what my Father had shown me in spite of the lack of support I received, but then there were the cloudy days when I, like the gainsayers, said to myself, "I must be crazy, who do I think I am anyway?" Satan loved those days. I remember sitting in front of my computer one day, thinking about a message that Bishop Smith had once preached called "My Day is Coming, But First." Before I could finish encouraging myself during this time of reflection, Satan changed the words of the sermon to "My Day is Coming, But When!" He is so slick isn't he? But he's also a sad little punk. The sad thing about the devil is that he forgets the real power of the dreamer. He forgets that the dreams that the Potter gives have the ability to remind you of who you can be aside from your reality. He forgets that whenever dreams are vivid, and repeated over and over again in your mind, they change from dreams into goals. Those goals then require you to take the next step in your faith which involves planning and writing your vision. Planning does not mean that you don't have faith, it means that you take your faith seriously. For a goal that has no plan is simply a wish, and not a goal at all. Our goals then if put in the proper perspective, can become a very real extension of our dream, and are what we are challenged to dwell on. This focus will ensure that we have the fortitude to take the next step toward making our dreams come true, which is inner commitment. Inner, by Webster's definition, means farther within or more secret. Commitment, the dictionary further explains, is to put into custody or prison; to bind as by promise. Your heart is the place of commitment. That is why the Word of God must be hidden there. What does this all mean? It means that the dreams, the goals you have in life and the commitment to it, only has to be inside of you. It means that no one else has to believe it and no one else has to see it. No one else even has to encourage it, for the Creator of the dream, the Giver of potential is all the cheerleader you need to make your vision come to pass.

The way has already been made; we just have to make our way to the Way.

A commitment to wholeness in our lives, to the dreams we have almost forgotten, and even to the relationships that we have, whether as parents, saints, servants, friends or life partners has to be deeply rooted in us. It needs to be so deeply rooted that the enemy of our souls, no matter what vehicle he uses, is unable to find it and rob us of it. Our hopes and dreams for everything and anything, have to be hidden with Christ in God. He is the only true resting place and the best there is at Hide and go Seek. Remember how in the childhood game, you were challenged to go find someone that was hidden from you? At times God's ways and the rationale behind what He does eludes us, but He has promised that if we will seek Him, we will find Him when we search for Him with all of our hearts. It is a direct connection to finding ourselves, when we find Him….when we learn Him. He assists us in making sense of the jigsaw puzzle and in holding onto our dreams. For whosoever seeks, He admonishes, finds, and to him that knocks, the door shall be opened. Then why is it that so many of us are asking, but not receiving? Could it be because we are really not seeking? Could it be because we lack the faith and patience that it takes to wait for this unseen God? The Psalmist David reminds us to be of good courage and wait on the Lord. We have mistaken this to mean that we should actually sit back and wait for the Lord to do something. But when I think of the word waitress or waiter which has wait as its root word, I realize that we have it all wrong. To wait is to attend to, to be at one's beck and call. To wait is to serve and not be served. Waiting on the Lord does not mean sitting back until He shows up. It means willingly making one's self available, even when there is no guarantee of compensation. The wait staff at your favorite restaurant knows that their service may be second to none, but that will not always result in the guarantee of a tip from a patron. Although the word tip means to insure proper service, a stingy patron may still withhold proper compensation for proper service. However, in spite of this, a good waitress or waiter walks into each situation blindly, diligent at their occupation, not knowing if they will be rewarded for it. If they love their job, they seek to please the patron due to their love for service and not simply in anticipation of reciprocity. It behooves us to serve our Father in the same way, not simply because of what we want Him to do for us, but because it is our pleasure to do so.

Joseph, my mentor, had gone through circumstance after circumstance that surely should have convinced him that what he had dreamed would never come to pass. Every since God had shown him his future and his destined place of promotion, there had been nothing but circumstantial evidence presented by his adversaries to convince him of his demotion and eventual demise. Joseph's challenge was rather to remember the fidelity of what God had revealed to him so many years before. His dream must have seemed like a horrible trick after seeing how his journey took him from the pit into slavery, betrayal and even to prison. The Potter's ways don't make sense and nothing seems to add up sometimes. He only asks though that you still trust His love for you, trust His Word, and trust that He really does have your best interest at heart. There have been times on this journey where I haven't believed that. "You care for me, is what they've told me all my life Lord, but I sure can't tell. Actions speak louder than words the old saying goes and right now, what you're showing me and what you're telling me in your Word are two different things." Whew! When I think of the "trash" talking that I have done to the Potter in recent years, I can't help but thank Him for His mercy and grace. Because of Jesus, we have a great High Priest who can be touched with the feelings of our infirmities, because He was in all points tempted as we are...Thank God! Otherwise, I would have been destroyed long ago, as I have been known to catch a major attitude with God concerning what He was allowing to take place in my life. At some of the twists and turns on my journey, I fussed at him because He seemed "bent" on making me unhappy. I vowed to Him that I would make my own happiness, with or without Him. How crazy we lumps of clay can be, but He so lovingly overlooks our idiotic episodes... thank you Jesus. He enables us to recapture our focus and love for Him. That love returns us to a place of adoration for Him, not because of what He does for us, but because of who He is to us.

Somehow as a dreamer, it never seemed to fail that whenever I was feeling my worse, nobody was there for me the way that I had tried to be there for other people. Well, I shouldn't say no one because the Lord was there, He was always there. And He knew exactly what that betrayal felt like. He knew exactly how much it hurt, to feel alone after giving so much of yourself to others. Wasn't it He who had healed the sick, raised the dead, gave hope, and poured out of Himself continuously during His three-year ministry, only to face Gethsemane and Calvary alone? No matter how well intended His disciples were, they had not been prepared for what He was about to face, nor could they support Him through it. There are moments when you will feel like an overdrawn checking account. People continue making withdrawals, forgetting or becoming too busy to deposit anything. Yet, they return again and again only to withdraw once more. Does anybody care that I'm all tapped out? It doesn't take long to grow weary of being available for other people's conveniences and happiness, while never having the same courtesies extended to you. But those feelings are only attempts to steal your dreams and your victory. That is why the Lord encourages us in His Word, saying "Come to me, all ye that are burdened and heavy laden and I will give you rest." He longs to provide for us what others are unable to provide. His healing gives you the ability, through it all, to dream again.

Remember Peter after the crucifixion? Jesus during His time with the disciples had taught them to dream of a better day. They'd seen the miracles and had enjoyed His presence. They looked forward to many more years together of service and friendship, only to be robbed of it all in the blink of an eye. Peter didn't know what to do. Up until now he had been so assured of who Jesus was and of what they were to do together as a team. Now He was gone, and to make matters worse, Peter had denied Him not just once, but three times. He knew nothing else to do but abandon his dream and return to fishing. It is our Jesus, the one I love so much, that stands on the shore as He watches Peter and the others fail at all attempts to catch fish. You see, this was no longer Peter's purpose in life. Jesus had promised Peter that if he followed Him, He would make him a fisher of men. It is evident here, how the frailty of our flesh at our low points, will convince us to go back to what is familiar instead of pressing toward what God has promised us. It is here that Jesus gives His beloved disciples the ability to try one more time as He commands them to cast their net onto the other side. Yes, they had toiled all night long to no avail, but because of the Word of the Potter, they were willing to try again.

My dear lumps of clay, always remember that it is not your option to give up on your dreams. It is the Dream Giver's good pleasure to give you the keys to the Kingdom, whatever the Kingdom represents in your life. However, you must constantly remind yourself that He has already given you those keys and has the specific instructions on what to do with them. His only requirement is that you be willing and obedient. But most of all, as the Author and Finisher of your faith, the destiny He has scripted for you also requires that you stay the dreamer that you are, and never ever let your faith fail!

CHAPTER VI

HELP WANTED

At some point in our lives, we all have been faced with the frightening and sometimes discouraging task of "pounding the pavement" in an attempt to find gainful employment. As we embark upon the tedious journey of combing the classified ads and internet job sites for some glimmer of hope, we are only aware of how much we personally need that job. We are not at all aware of the effects that the vacant position has had on the now possibly desperate employer, and the employees who were left behind.

Never had I realized the impact of this until recently when our receptionist happily moved on to another place of employment to pursue her interests. My co-workers and I were then tasked with the awesome responsibility of having to fill her shoes while simultaneously handling our personal workloads as well. She had moved on, and therefore had no knowledge of the chaos that she'd left behind.

In the beginning, I was very angry at my boss for this. It wasn't as if she hadn't given proper notice and ample time to find her replacement. We'd received dozens of resumes, emails, and phone calls regarding the position. Yet after more than a month, there seemed to me, no true effort given to filling the position. Not once had it dawned on me that perhaps the manager and owner were simply unable to find the qualified person that we were so desperately in need of. That person of balance, who not only possessed administrative skill, but one that could bring love and passion to the position, yet provide loyalty and longevity to the agency as well.

As if to add insult to injury, to my dismay, another key employee left for a week of scheduled vacation in the midst of all the disarray. Needless to say, as a new employee myself, I began to experience a week of absolute frustration and stress. It was not until the end of that very trying week that the Holy Spirit allowed me to see the spiritual implications of this very common event. How devastating it must be to the Kingdom when we resign from our extremely vital positions as servants, lights, and witnesses. For various reasons, we become so engrossed with the pursuit of our own personal goals and agendas that we forget the reason we were hired in the first place.

Paul admonishes us in the book of II Timothy, the 4th chapter, to do the work of an evangelist. What does that really mean? Webster's dictionary describes an evangelist as one who zealously preaches the gospel or converts others to Christianity. However, I propose that this is not the person whom we see preaching on television, or even the person that runs your church's annual revival. A true evangelist is one who allows the Father to model His magnificent glory while performing their normal life's duties on a daily basis. The one who seeks opportunities to make a difference in the midst of whatever circumstance or situation they have been assigned to. It is not always scriptures quoted, but love, acceptance, balance and calm brought to the lives of those that come into contact with you from day to day.

Evangelism means not being so "bogged" down with your own plight and personal problems that you can't be an encouragement to those around you. Take a look around you, where you work, who you work with, and the clients you serve. Nothing is by accident. You only know the individuals that you know because they were assigned to your "watch" before time even began. Have you let them down? Have those whose lives you were assigned to impact, missed their day of visitation due to your preoccupation with your own life?

Paul deals with our urgency to win souls in II Corinthians 5:11. He says, "Knowing therefore the terror of the Lord, we persuade others." If you are like me, you have oftentimes been too mesmerized by the distractions in your life to persuade others to follow the true meaning of life, Jesus Christ. Therefore, if you are off duty, who will be the beacon that your friend, co-worker, neighbor, manager, or company needs?

In my mind's eye, I have imagined that the Lord would write a classified ad in search of willing workers that goes something like this:

"HELP WANTED"

<u>Kingdom Laborer</u>

Experience preferred, but willing to train.
Must be strong, courageous, cunning in
Warfare and prayer. Seeking one who is virtuous,
Walks in wisdom, and has the ability to speak grace & truth
fluently in love. The applicant's light must shine brightly.

All busybodies, tattlers, meddlers in other men's matters, lazy and cowards need not apply.

It sounds comical at first glance doesn't it? But in reality, I find that the kingdom is definitely short of dedicated laborers. Sure we have many who attend church faithfully and lay claim to the title of Christian, but we don't have enough sold out soldiers who will live sacrificially. The life of a disciple/warrior/laborer of Jesus Christ is an unselfish one. A life of ups and downs, highs and lows, good days and bad days. A succession of thousands of encounters all equaling up to one heck of a journey.

I submit to you, my fellow lumps of clay that the reason why the harvest is still so plenteous, is because the true laborers are still so few. To be a laborer is not necessarily a glamorous job. At times you will have to bear the heat of the day for very little pay. At times it will seem as though you have given too much only to receive too little in return.

As a result of this the so-called laborers of the gospel spend way too much time asking the Potter/Husbandman of the harvest why, when we really should be asking what? What would you have me to be doing right now Father? We should be seeking daily instruction, but some of us have reduced ourselves to either weekly or monthly inquiries of God's itinerary for our lives. We are readily able to accept that our natural jobs and employers may require a variety of demands for our time and attention. And although these requests may be given with no consideration of our inconvenience as employees, and may change at any given time, we accept these responsibilities hoping to keep our much needed jobs and impress the watchful eye of our superiors. We are open and flexible to the request of other mere humans, while we are not nearly as apt to be concerned about what is on our Potter's daily agenda or List of Things to Do. Something to think about, isn't it?

I have finally come to a point in my life where what others want me to do is not nearly as important to me as what the Potter wants me to do. There have been several occasions where I have had to obey what I felt He was leading me to do although no one else could understand what I was doing. I had to remember that His sheep know His voice and a stranger they will not follow. I learned the true meaning of what Peter meant when he feared the stormy sea, but yet replied "Lord if it is you bid me to come." Many times the bidding of the Lord and my faith that He would hold me up was all I had to go on. It is my belief that the Potter honors this type of faith and will not disappoint it. Each time I have moved, based on His instruction, I have experienced a peace that you would not believe. Knowing that you are in God's will and have accepted His "orders" for your life is a place of rest like no other. There may be signs of uncertainty, doubt and unbelief from those closest to you, but you must be determined to love and trust your Potter more than you do yourself, or those around you.

Some years ago, I went to the theatre to see the new movie "Mission Impossible." It was a remake of the very popular television series from the 1970's. Although I remember watching it as a child, I do not remember always understanding everything that went on during the program. I specifically recall, however, that every episode seemed to be jammed pack with danger, suspense and espionage.

Each week, the tape which held instructions for the secret agent, always disintegrated once the assignment was given. In retrospect, I now realize that the tape would disintegrate for two reasons. First, because the instructions detailed were for the ears of that agent only. Secondly, because once the assignment was finished, there would be no time to relish in the victories of the last assignment, as there would be a new challenge assigned. As I sat through scene after scene in this movie remake, there was one statement that continued to resonate in my ears even long after I'd left the movie theatre that night. Just prior to the tape disintegrating, the voice stated with what seemed to me to be such conviction and passion, "this is your assignment if you choose to accept it." My God!!! I was probably the only person in the universe that had been so deeply impacted by this one statement, but I couldn't shake it. I continued to hear this voice for days in my mind. It only got louder and louder with time…KATRINA, THIS IS YOUR MISSION IF YOU CHOOSE TO ACCEPT IT!! As a result of that voice, I now understand that everything the Potter has designed for you as His lump of clay, must be accepted by you. It is a choice to yield to the Potter and the orders that He assigns to your footsteps. Oftentimes the acceptance of His will for your life will predispose you to some of the most detestable locations and circumstances. But here is where your "Not my will but thy will" of Gethsemane should kick into play. A yielded servant chooses to accept their assignment, even given the most dismal conditions, because he understands that there is a war to be won and justice to be served. Can the Potter count on you to accept His mission of reaching the lost at any cost, or do you have too many other things to do?

GOD'S REASON
(Author Unknown)

I don't know how to say it
But somehow it seems to me
That maybe we are stationed,
Exactly where God wants us to be.
That little place we're filling
Is the reason for our birth,
And just to do the work we do,
He sent us down to earth.
If God had nothing otherwise,
I reckon He'd have made
Each one of us a little different
Of a worse or better grade;
And since God knows and understands
All things of land and sea,
I fancy that He placed us here,
Just where He wanted us to be.
Sometimes we get to thinking,

As our labors we review,
That we should like a higher place
With greater things to do;
But we come to the conclusion
When the envying is stilled,
That the post to which God sent us
Is the post He wanted filled.
And there isn't any service
We should scoff or we should scorn,
For it may be just the reason
God allowed us to be born.

CHAPTER VII
IT'S A THIN LINE

There is an old adage that says, "There's a thin line between love and hate". Surely the person who coined this phrase had experienced some serious consequences and repercussions which brought them to this resolve. I, just like the unknown author of this quote, have had life's lesson teach me the same. There is indeed a thin line between love and hate. For it is the same one that makes your heart flutter, skip a beat, and feel as though it could fly away on clouds, that also has the ability to make that same heart feel as though it has been run over by a 18-wheeler tractor trailer.

Have you ever had the experience of expecting a phone call from the one you love? Jumping each time the phone rings, waiting with baited breath, hoping it's them and completely exuberant about simply another opportunity to hear his or her voice once again. Only to have that same person call you a week later, and the day happen to be preceded by a minor misunderstanding. Now as the phone rings, you sigh, roll your eyes, look at the caller ID and struggle with yourself as to whether you should pick up the phone or let it go to voicemail? When it comes to matters of the heart, my fellow lumps of clay, isn't it funny how fickle the emotions can be? We can be madly in love one week and insanely wishing we had never even met a person the following week. Many of you may have never experienced this thin line and perhaps it would be better for you if you hadn't. However, if you have experienced this flip flop of the heart at some point in time, it may be easier for you to wrap your mind around the idea that I am about to share with you.

On my journey I experienced a type of thin line such as this with my Father, the Potter. I've gone from loving what He's doing with my life to absolutely hating what He's doing with it, and have at times wished He would just leave me alone! Some of you reading may want to act surprised that I would even express such a thing openly, but this book is not about lying to yourself, others or the Lord. It's about a true journey with plenty of bumps, bruises, disappointments and conflicts. There's been an abundance of fist shaking at God as I reprimanded Him for doing the total opposite of what I wanted done. However, I find that my true "love Jones" for Him always sends me running back to Him. Or maybe it's really His love Jones for me that actually **brings** me back to Him. He always has this way with me that makes me remember why I fell in love with Him in the first place. Any real man can do this with ease you know, and Jesus is definitely the real deal.

My soul has often time been in conflict, weary from being kicked around by life, wondering how much more of this the Lord would allow me to take, and what kind of love was this to stand by and watch me get beat up so badly? Then I remembered the beat down that the Father allowed His Son to take for me. It reminded me of the words that Jesus spoke in St. John 15:13 "Greater love hath no man than this, that a man lay down his life for his friends." At those times when I had to lay down what it was that I wanted, and allow what it was that He wanted, my heart could only relay these words to the Potter of His treatment regarding His lump of clay, "I don't understand you, but I love you".

My re-evaluation and reassessment of my relationship with the Lord has uncovered for me the realization that there is not only a thin line between love and hate when it comes to your spiritual and natural relationships, but there is also a thin line between God and good. Just what do I mean by that? Well, a few spins on the Potter's wheel, while trying to do it my way, has shown me that what may be good, does not always resemble what God has in mind for **you**. In other words, to the natural eye, or from the outside looking in, something could seem like a wonderful idea, a good strategic move. But when God has purpose lined up for your life, it is very critical that you move according to His cadence and always in His season. Otherwise it is very easy for you to wander off onto your own path thinking that because you're doing good things, God must be pleased. We have a way of rationalizing the decisions and moves that we have made, even when we know that we have done so without receiving proper instruction from the Potter. Although you may be doing a good deed, if it is not what is on His agenda for you at this present time, you are crossing that thin line. It is not only sin that we must be aware of as followers of His voice, but also our own will, desire, and need for approval, and promotion. These feelings and desires are mere byproducts of our flesh. They are not things that are sinful in and of themselves, but they can be detrimental to our lives as obedient servants, when they are not brought under the submission of the will of our Father.

Remember my fellow lumps of clay that God is not in as much of a hurry as you and I are. He is faithful that promised. He is also longsuffering that promised and He is patient that promised. He does not become anxious and nervous just because we do. Your blessings? Your elevation? All in His timing, for "He knows the thoughts that He thinks towards you….thoughts of peace and not of evil, to give you an expected end." (Jeremiah 29:11) Trust that, and be careful not to cross the thin line between love and hate, or God and good. The Potter has already "peeped" your destiny and He has your best interest at heart. Know that! Even when the enemy tries to convince you otherwise. The love of God upon your life doesn't change nor does the favor of God upon your life change. But, you must wait patiently for the highs and the lows of His voice, being sure not to mistake your intellect for His will.

Modern technology has a new way of formulating passwords. This technology allows your recorded voice to be the means by which you gain access into company files and software. It memorizes not only your voice, but your voice's depth, highs, lows, pitch, etc., which are difficult to duplicate. This unique form of identification prevents access of valuable information to an unauthorized user, an imposter if you will. In your life, the Potter's voice and your recognition of it, must become this distinct to you. His guidance is essential for your journey. DO NOT GET AHEAD OF HIM! The Holy Spirit is the "scout" for your soul. He has already been briefed by the Potter as to what your life is destined to be, and if you will be sensitive to His leading, He will escort you directly to the breach that needs your anointing. Never again use as a scapegoat "I am helping a lot of people, so God must be in it" or "this is a good thing, so it must be God." The line is too thin between God and good, so know your God, and know the unique sound of His voiceprint. Doing so will not only bless your life, but it will save you a lot of unnecessary heartache.

CHAPTER VIII
SAVED, SINGLE & UNSATISFIED

I can remember browsing the Christian bookstore looking for some type of encouragement that would shake me from the despondent mood that I'd found myself suddenly in. As I browsed books written by famous authors, moderators and preachers of the Gospel, I remember seeing a book entitled "Saved, Single & Satisfied," and wondering what was wrong with me. Yes I was saved, I was single, but I definitely was not satisfied. I'd grown tired of attending every function alone, bearing every burden alone, and making every life decision alone. There was no one to share the responsibility of raising my young children with.

It has been said in the past that attitude determines altitude. I am afraid, that this popular cliché has become nothing more than that. However, I am convinced by not just my own experiences, but the experiences of others, that this really is not just another cliché. Your attitude tremendously affects your state of mind, which has a domino effect, thereby affecting your situation. Not only does it effect it, but it will either minister life or death to that situation. The Bible says that out of the abundance of the heart, the mouth speaks. Therefore, even the words you speak reflect the attitude that abides in your heart concerning yourself and others. Words are powerful yes, but words emanate from inside of us, from what we believe to be true about ourselves. We often pray that our conditions will change or that our desires will be met, when what we really need to be praying is that our attitudes will be adjusted, and the emotions that are produced from them will change.

Attitude is even more important than physical beauty. Think about it, the appearance of a container can advertise a good product. Yes, marketing does count, but it's the picture on the box or jar that entices you to buy the item. It is, in fact, the contents of the package that keeps you, the consumer, coming back time and time again to buy that product. We spend so much time, especially as women, trying to impress people with what is seen only by the physical eye. But we forget that what can be seen is only the wrapping. It is not an indication of what the inside of a person is like. Somewhere in this world is another person who needs exactly what's on the inside of you. The book of Psalms so eloquently states that the King's daughters are all glorious within. I don't want to alienate the men by using this scripture, but I would like to remind my sisters in Christ of how much time the Potter took to divinely decorate you inwardly with His glory. A beauty that no amount of makeup or designer clothing can provide.

God is able to send the person into your life that appreciates you, and everything about you. But until he or she arrives, you must learn to appreciate who and what God has made you. More often than not, we aren't able to find our self-worth from God's Word and His love alone. We usually don't feel loved or wanted until another human being loves and wants us. When it is the Lord who loves you and wants you regardless of the kind of shape you're in. He has seen you at your worst and has never held it against you. His friendship has been consistent, and because you are valuable to God, you have all the value and validation that you'll ever need.

At the beginning of this book, I asked the question "Why hast thou made me thus?" It is a question that I have posed to the Potter at several different intervals along my journey. I had to overcome what I call the single woman's plight, that feeling that because I was single, I must not be worth someone's love and attention. I didn't understand that there was a reason that I'd been honored with the call of singleness. An honor you say Katrina? Yes, an honor that sometimes feels like the pits, but an honor that taught me how to be whole and complete within myself. Sometimes, although you survive the hurt and robbery that accompanies past relationships, you lose a substantial degree of your self esteem. You begin to feel as though everyone else has somebody, so what's wrong with me? If I'm so pretty and so much fun to be with, why am I alone? Listen, I am an observer of people and as such there have been many times that I would sit in my office and watch couples come and go. I'd see fat women, skinny women, raggedy women, bald women, hairy women WALK IN WITH HUSBANDS!!!! All I could think was okay God what is wrong with this picture? What is the problem? How can SHE get a husband looking like that, and I can't???? I'll tell you what the problem is. You cannot pattern your life by what God has done in other people's lives. He knows exactly what path you should have taken. Why you were left, deserted, rejected or just alone. So don't allow yourself to agonize over what **YOU** see as tragedy, and begin to understand that for every struggle that you endured, another brick went into the building of your character. It takes a lot more fortitude and tenacity to endure a plane crash than it does to survive one. A very good friend of mine taught me that you survive by chance, but you endure by choice. Another valuable lesson that life has taught me is that you can't allow your personal opinions, or the opinions of others, to determine what is appropriate for your life. We have a way of setting timetables that God has nothing to do with, because of what our friends, family members or even we have convinced ourselves of.

I remember how I would complain about what I couldn't do for God because I was married. Then once my husband divorced me, after about a year of being alone, I thought to myself, "Hey! This is inconvenient, I need a covering". I thought that I needed an outside source to make me happy, not realizing that my happiness had to come from within me. Otherwise, I could not be complimentary to my new mate once he did arrive. I would be a subtraction, a complication, and not a true helpmeet, needing to draw from my significant other, rather than add to him.
It is important that we master the lessons that the Potter will teach us during our singleness. Marriage, if that is His choice for us, will not be blissful by osmosis. It will,

however, be fulfilling if you are attentive to your class time with God during your time of singleness. What you will learn from the Potter about selflessness, obedience, submission and yes, most importantly unconditional love, will definitely prepare you for your mate.

Honesty is key in your quest for satisfaction with your singleness. You must be honest enough to confront yourself with the question of whether you would compliment someone's life or complicate it. If you are a whiner, a very critical or judgmental person, this time of singleness, is a time to work on that. You see, to marry someone, means that you will marry their strengths and their weaknesses. It means that you must be a good team mate and a good partner. You won't tear the person down because of their weaknesses, but you emphasize their strengths and stand in the gap where there is weakness. Partnership is responsibility, the ability to respond in any situation. Therefore, it is vital that you become your partner's biggest coach, fan, cheerleader, and confidant. Able to prove that it matters not how much money they make, what type of car they drive, how fine they are, or even how imperfect they are. What matters most is your assigned destiny into this person's life. What matters most is the ability to celebrate life, and all that life holds with someone who makes you feel as though you can accomplish anything.

Sadly enough, if you view marriage as an opportunity to just make you happy, you have already started out on the wrong foot, and are destined for disaster. You cannot and should not look for someone to complete you and complete your life. You must possess completion before they enter your life, otherwise you will be setting the relationship up for failure. Saved, single **AND** satisfied? Yes it is possible, it is doable, even if not always our first choice. Satisfaction with singleness is attainable and the state of being unmarried does not have to be considered as some sort of death sentence. Embrace it, and cherish it as your preparation time, and your pampering time. Your time of service to others, and your time of undivided attention to the desires of your Potter. Singleness can be a blessing when you look at it through the right set of eyelids….

CHAPTER IX
THAT'S WHAT FRIENDS ARE FOR

Singer, songwriter R. Kelly wrote a song some years back titled "I Believe I Can Fly". The inspiration that echoed throughout the lyrics of this song had to stem from Mr. Kelly's "God-given" talent, but most emphatically from a "God-given" message. I don't think there is anyone that's ever heard this song that wasn't, at some point in time, touched and encouraged by Robert Kelly's plea for our perseverance. He reminds us not only of our need to believe that we can touch the sky, but that we should think about it every night and day. How we should just spread our wings and fly away. It is this comparison to a bird's flight, that my mind's eye needed in order to escort me to a place where my faith could take me. Above where my circumstances had positioned me. He continues to admonish that if "we believe that we can soar, we can see ourselves running through any open door".

I am convinced that seeing ourselves achieving our dream is imperative and also required if we are to live in the reality of that same dream. Often while on this journey of the Potter's wheel, I have found myself simultaneously in the lowest of valleys. Having had numerous doors close in my face, betrayed, and disillusioned by the seemingly endless amount of games and politics that people play both inside and outside of the church. It has seemed impossible at times to believe that I could fly. Sometimes I didn't even feel like trying to fly anymore. I could no longer find the energy to be hopeful, upbeat or optimistic about my future. I thought about the unthinkable, "just give up Katrina" I told myself. A thought that the tenacious and "Wonder Woman" like Katrina, would have frowned upon and never fathomed. To put it simply, my wings, the wings of my mind that R. Kelly sang about, just felt as if they were broken. After so much disappointment in life, the weight of being a fighter my whole life had begun to take an effect on my wings. There is no feeling quite as disheartening as the feeling of believing that you have been disappointed by God, and by the choices that you have made. It is amazing how adversely those emotions can affect your eyesight. Suddenly, I couldn't see myself soaring or running through any open doors. Suddenly, I felt betrayed by my closest friend, Jesus. My eyes began to play tricks on me, and it seemed as if God Himself was now the culprit. He was, in fact, the one standing on the other side of those supposed open doors, slamming them time after time in my face. Doing nothing to bring the type of relief that I thought I needed, as life was busy kicking and slapping me around mercilessly. Should we be disappointed with the Potter? Of course we shouldn't, we know that! But it is the voice of our adversary that taunts us, and shouts louder than what we know in our hearts to be true whenever we feel our lowest. It is he that accuses our Heavenly Father of lack of love and support, as he pummels us with questions of "Is this how God repays you for serving Him? Is this what you get for following what you believed to be His voice? Is this the thanks you get for all you've sacrificed to live for Him?" These are the "below the belt" blows that Satan uses as opportunities to take advantage of us over time, because he knows when we've grown weary in the fight for our faith.

I'd heard it said before that friends are like angels who help you to fly when your own wings seem unable to do so. And it was at those times that my Father, knowing my true love for Him, yet understanding my weariness in battle, has sent His comfort to me in the form of my friends. I call them my "Sistas"! These are my girls, my homies, my soul sistas. I spell sista with an "a" because it is different from the word sister. Since we were not born of the same mother, the same blood does not run through our veins. We are, however, born of the same father, our Heavenly Father, therefore the same blood actually does runs through our veins. These are my sisters in Christ, my blood washed sisters, walking along with me on this sometimes tedious journey. Their presence and encouragement was there with me, even when they could not literally walk my walk with me, or for me. Loving me and accepting me unconditionally, as if they had known me my whole life. We have laughed together, cried together, prayed together, raised children together, pursued careers together, gone back to school together, lost jobs together, been looked over for promotions together, and been hurt and/or deserted by people that said they loved us together. All…together.

When I was a little girl growing up in Brooklyn, New York, there was a game that my friends and I would play with our jump ropes. I don't even remember what the game was actually called, but as an adult when I reflect back on it today, the song that we would sing reminds me of the true essence of sisterhood. Two girls would turn the rope, and then one of my friends would jump into the rope. Once she jumped in, the rest of us would start chanting

"All, all, all, all" until every other girl would join the first girl, jumping in one at a time. Although at times it seemed like we were saying "all, all" for an eternity, as we painstakingly waited for each girl to feel confident enough to take the leap and jump in, we would patiently wait for each girl every single time. Once we were all "in", we would continue singing "all in together girls, how you like the weather girls? January, February, March", and so on until we had called out all the months of the year. As each girl's birthday month was called, she would jump out of the rope, with skill and great care in order to ensure that she did not mess up the tempo, turning of the rope, or timing of the other girls as she exited.

I would ask you to revisit with me if you will, the phrase "all in together girls, how you like the weather girls?" How do I like the weather girls? Well, there have been many days that I absolutely hated the weather. There were cloudy days, rainy days, thunderous days, tornado-like days, hurricane days, and rarely, yes never often enough, sunny days. But it's funny that on the same day that it may have been partly sunny for me, it might have been a torrential rain day for one of my sistas. However, we were still "all in together girls". Just like in the childhood game, we waited for each other. Whenever one was hurting, all were hurting. We couldn't stop whatever was going on in our individual lives, just like we couldn't stop turning that rope, but we could rally around whichever sista was having problems with the ups and downs of life and wait for her to jump back in when she felt ready. Always keeping her mindful, yet hopeful of our desire for her to "catch up" with our silent chants of "all, all, all, all, all in together girls".

My journey has forever been impacted by these specially assigned and designed angels from above. Some of them I see every day, others of them I only see every once in a while, yet the blessing they have been to my life is evident all around me. None of them are alike in personality, but all of them have a piece of me inside of them, and I carry a piece of them inside of me as well.

There must be one who always reminds you to laugh at yourself, and the things that are going wrong in your life. Laugh at it all she consistently has shown me down through the years. Your mess-ups, your hang-ups, your phobias, and your crazy family problems. She teaches me to always appreciate the wonder of the Potter's world. His flowers, His trees, His birds, His beautiful blue sky, and yes, even

His rain. I make fun of her at times, as she rants about the craziness of her children, her out of control ovaries, and her out of touch husband, while in the same sentence she gives praise to the Father as she veers off into one of her "cosmic mother earth" tangents. But I need that, I need all of that from her. Why? Because she's shown me how to laugh at it all, instead of cry for it all. The delight that she sees in creation refreshes my memory of the genius that is my Father. Surely if He has provided for the birds of the air, there is no doubt that He will provide for me. After all, why wouldn't He? He actually died for me, and what greater love is there than that?

Then there's the sista that loves a challenge, and whose energy seems to know no bounds. She is loud, full of life, full of giggles, and always ready to hit the road. Whether it is time to shop 'til you drop, or cry over spilled milk, she is on ready, set, go. Willing to be whatever, or to go wherever you need. She is my reminder to live life to the fullest, no matter what's going on around you. Get out and dance like there's nobody watching. She never parks by her disappointments, she moves on to the next thing that can bring her joy. She teaches me about forgiveness, acceptance, and unconditional love. My sista teaches me the courage, and fortitude that it takes to keep it moving....no matter what. To never give bitterness, or discouragement a home in my heart....she teaches me that happy circumstances are not the criteria for joy.

Now I move on to the sista who is the "Quiet Storm". Her aura is unassuming, non-provoking, non-threatening, and almost passive. She is soft & warm, a gentle rose whose thorns surface only when there is the danger of being trampled underfoot by an unworthy admirer. She teaches me to never mistake meekness for weakness. She teaches me that it is okay to be humble, it just is not okay to allow yourself to be humiliated. You rise above it, you rise above it all. Even when your opposition seems bigger, stronger, wiser, and in control, you trust God to assist you in your reminder to them that you will be controlled only by your Potter. I've watched her transition from the one whose happiness was at the mercy of another, to being the one from whom mercy had to be requested. She went from the "hunted" to a "hurricane" in her own quiet way. Maintaining her class, daintiness, and ability to re-invent herself; She is my role model, for she teaches me that it is alright to have to start all over again from scratch, and that you owe explanations to no one for needing to do so.

What can adequately be said of my feisty little "Sista Momma"? The sista who is also your mother? She is your greatest cheerleader, perpetually raising those pom-poms in the air, leading the parade for you whatever your pursuit in life. You can almost hear her chanting "Pooh Bear, Pooh Bear, she's our man, if she can't do it no one can!" She is my faith in me when I am unable to find my own. Like a bear to her baby cub, she is protector, teacher, friend, advocate, and greatest admirer. My determination is rejuvenated by her belief in the beauty of the vision for my life that the Potter has given to me.

" Sista Rough Around The Edges", I can't leave you out. It is hard for some to see the commonality between you and me. Your exterior screams out that you are surely one of those who has lost your way. Yet, I see your inward man striving to carve out your personal niche in the world. Never giving up until you've made your contribution for the betterment of whatever entity you are assigned to. You teach me to never make excuses for falling short. To own up to my shortcomings, and somehow find the strength to reach beyond them to the potential that lies within me. I see within you the same will of a warrior that I see in me.

Always willing to sacrifice your comfort and convenience for the goal of a better day. You are a champion, consistently unwilling to allow the bumps and bruises of previous ill choices to rob you of the healing power that rests in your ability to never quit. You have mastered the art of being yourself in spite of your critics, of never being afraid to dust yourself off and give it another shot! So thank you my friend for your demonstration of what it truly means to be a wounded healer.

Sista Madea! What can adequately be said to describe your unique "ride or die" love? Your marshmallow-like interior, and maternal instincts are guised beneath a tough exterior of all day, every day I'm a thug tendencies. I'm so honored to be one of the few allowed close enough to experience the secret essence of your gentle kindness, your heart's compassion for our children, and the depth of your commitment to those that you love and care about. I've learned from you how to cry about my past, but how to fight not to repeat it. How to fight for the destiny of my children as I balance being their strongest critic, yet simultaneously their loudest cheerleader. Without question, I am a more loving and attentive mother in conjunction with providing the discipline necessary, especially for my son in the absence of a father in the home all because of you. I didn't always understand the balance of those two responsibilities, and how needful both roles were to my children. You redirected me by your example of how I could be the gentle nurturer that the Potter intended me to be, yet the strong arm of the law when circumstances deemed me to be. Your will and determination have inspired me, and even when you didn't know it, I was paying close attention, watching how you handled the ugly hand that had been dealt to you. You looked at the hand, saddened by what you saw, you talked to our Father and made the decision to take no prisoners and exceed everyone's expectations. You took me into your class room and lovingly gave me the education that I didn't even realized I'd been lacking. And it is for these lessons my sista, my friend that I am most grateful.

Does anybody have a Sista"Tell It Like It Is"? Where would I be without you in my life? Militant, take no prisoners, love me or hate me, it really doesn't matter, that's the Woman of God that you are. You force us to see things as they really are, not as we desire for them to be. Truth is your greatest attribute. You cut us with it, and then you heal us with that same truth. Your love for life never overshadows your love for the Father. You are to the fullest extent an evangelist, yet full fledged "thug" simultaneously. I love to watch you work. I sit quietly and watch you in awe as you flow from preacher to comedienne, then to loving mother and wife, purposed sister and faithful friend. The songwriter sang it best, You're Every Woman". Big Sista, it's ALL in you. No airs…no lies…no fronts. "I'm angry, I'm hurt, I'm sad, I'm fat, I'm hungry, I'm happy, I'm cussin' you out, I'm lovin' you up!" You're subject to say any of it, or all of it at any given time. It's all there, out on the table, what reason is there for hiding or holding back? You pour wisdom into the very core of our thirsty, parched souls from your pitcher of life. Your stories play out for us the gut-wrenching, heartbreaking, earth shattering experiences of your own life, as you personally extend to each of us the part of us that we honestly need to see. The part of us that we need to embrace is not the only component exposed, but the segments of us that need to be eradicated are also brought to light. You teach us that there can be no healing, nor can there be any restoration until there is forgiveness. I've learned that at times, forgiveness has more to do with what **I did or didn't do**, instead of dwelling on what was done to me. I am humbled as I reflect on what trouble I would be in if the Potter were to use all that I've done wrong against me in a court of law. You've taught me that mercy insists that I don't nurse another's indiscretions, dusting them off like trophies for display whenever I need to feel superior or self-righteous. What if my Father pulled my mistakes out like some trump card whenever He wanted to show me why things were in the mess they're in? How it was all my fault that He hadn't blessed me as I thought He should. As humans, we are often quick to judge other's shortcomings. Wearing the scars that unfaithful husbands, two-faced girlfriends, and back-stabbing church members have left us with across our chest as if they were some badge of honor to be applauded and recognized. This is our reminder to ourselves as well as to the Potter that the reason we are the way we are is because of what THEY DID TO US!!!

Well, this sista, wise counselor that she is, carefully navigates her students away from our self-centered rampages of self pity via her own unique style of counseling session. Her classes are usually conducted while donning pajamas, head scarves, and sipping numerous cups of coffee. With sleep sometimes dancing on our eyelids, we anxiously await the morsels of knowledge that will comically drop from her lips. She meticulously steers us away from the pain of what was done to us each and every time that we attempt to re-visit that sore spot, back to the focus of what could have, or should have been done by us to produce a different and more desired result. I walked away from class most recently reminded that I have a responsibility both to myself and to my Heavenly Father to forgive, AND TO FORGET as He has so often done for me. "Sista Tell It Like It Is", you are the epitome of the woman in the book of Proverbs, who through wisdom builds her house. As you illustrate to us through your own trial and error, that only a fool pulls down her house with her own hands. So thank you Sista, for your insight has guided me to the true essence of joy in life. That there is no greater realm of happiness than love of God, love of family, the sanctity of friendship, and the bond of honest, sincere, unconditional sisterhood. Yes, I feel as if I must say it once more, truly that's what friends are for!

CHAPTER X
I'M A WARRIOR, SATURATE ME!

Webster's Dictionary defines a warrior as one who fights in a war or battle. Other synonyms are used as well such as, fighter, soldier, mercenary, combatant. I personally would venture to go even a little further and add the word champion to that list of synonyms. In other words, one who never stops fighting; one who never gives up. As a young girl growing up in the projects of Brooklyn, New York, when I prepared for school in the morning I would listen to an old AM/FM radio that sat on top of the medicine cabinet in our bathroom. This radio was older than I was I think, and therefore couldn't pick up any of the popular urban or R&B radio stations that I would have preferred to listen to. Due to the absence of an antenna, and the sheer logistics of our bathroom, our entertainment system was forced to be more of an AM radio than FM. This meant that I was only able to listen to a lot of Soft Rock and Pop Rock while starting my day instead of the types of music that my teenage counterparts were listening to. Because of this exposure, although partially against my will, I heard a song one day by Queen that I immediately fell in love with, and I still love to this day. I didn't know at the time why this song inspired me so, but it was as if it lighted something up inside me every time I would hear it. The words say "We are the champions my friends, and we'll keep on fighting 'til the end. We are the champions, we are the champions! No time for losers, for we are the champions of the world." I didn't know at the time that this song would almost become my silent battle cry as I would enter into adulthood. Over and over again, I've found myself in various stages of war, having to remind myself of my championship status. Having the heart of a champion is just as much a choice as it is innate. For there will be several opportunities during your life's journey that you'll feel justified in simply giving up. You will convince yourself that you have done all that you could do, and that you cannot take even one more step. This is why the Apostle Paul, one of God's most awesome generals admonishes us to fight the good fight of faith and lay hold on eternal life.

Does the Potter not compare this life to a race when He tells us in His Word that the battle is not given to the swift, nor to the strong, but to he that endures to the end? Therefore it is safe to say that the Potter understands warfare perfectly, for the bible even describes the Lord as a man of war. Perhaps this is why He inspires Paul to write regarding our unique weaponry when he states in I Corinthians that "the weapons of our warfare are not carnal, but mighty through God." He speaks of a war that cannot be won with guns, weapons of mass destruction, or even our will and emotions. He writes to young Timothy as a father in the gospel, and encourages him to "endure hardness as a good soldier of Jesus Christ". He reminds Timothy that no one who wars has time to be entangled with life's affairs if he is to please the one that called him to be a soldier. Can you imagine a soldier in Iraq losing his concentration on the front line by taking time to wonder about whether his wife paid the electricity bill last Tuesday, or if the kids remembered to walk the dog? His current state deems that he must perform as if the outside world does not even exist if he is to complete the mission assigned to him with precision and minimum loss of life. He can't choose the heat of battle to reflect upon his children's chores, his monthly obligations, or even to reminisce about the comforts of home like Sunday dinner, a nice hot shower, or a long, hard night of the "couch potato work-out". He must stay focused and endure the present hardship as if it is the only life that he knows. The word endurance implies then that there is a choice involved. You have the option of being AWOL, absent without leave as a soldier, or remaining to fight until the death. What will you choose to do?

In sports, I've personally watched a few championship playoffs in the world of basketball and football. I am not a consistent viewer during regular season play, but there has always been something about the playoffs that peaks my interest. I believe it is the passion of the players involved as they scratch and fight to be named the best in the league. I've watched men play in spite of torn ligaments, sprained ankles, stomach flues, dehydration, and broken fingers just to name a few. I've seen them play in downpours of rain, and snow falling so heavily that it was difficult to even see where goal lines were. All because of a hunger in their spirits to beat the best of the best. Where is it that you learn that type of fervor? Are you born with it? Is it taught to you by a coach or given to you by your Creator? It is my belief that it is first given to you by your Creator, the Potter and can only be nurtured by a coach or mentor assigned to you by Him. Either way whether it is taught, instilled, or innate, I know that I must have it. It's not enough to just make the team, I must go home with the championship ring! After all, what is my excuse? I have all of Heaven cheering me on.

For you see, warriors don't settle for the easy road, but they almost intuitively seem to take the road less traveled. That is why the presence of God's anointing is so vital to them. It is often that a true warrior is venturing into unknown territory, but venture on he or she knows they must. They are not just civil service employees, working side by side with the active duty personnel on the base. Oh no, a warrior is quite the contrary. For unlike their civil servant counterparts, who may be assigned to the same military base, receive a paycheck from the same Department of Defense, and enjoy health care rendered at the same base hospitals and dental clinics, it is the active duty personnel AKA warrior who is willing however to lay his life on the line as a part of his commitment to his employer. Warriors, simply said, have a different set of "orders" that they must adhere to. The responsibility is greater, and so is the sacrifice. For you see, a warrior would rather die fighting than stagnantly or idly enjoy longevity. If you don't believe me, just ask Goliath's David which one he would rather have been.

If you've ever known someone in the military, it is strange to watch their response to receiving orders to the battlefield. There isn't this kicking and screaming sort of response (well for the most part), which is what the average person's response would be at the thought of facing impending danger and potential death. They have quite the opposite reaction, exuding a unique sense of calmness as they remind themselves possibly, and those that they love that this is what they are paid to do.

Perhaps this almost eerie sense of duty and responsibility stems from the intensive boot camp training, and/or ongoing leadership training that they are exposed to as they progress in their military career. I'm not sure which it is attributed to, but I am convinced that there are several things that these warriors have learned along the way that makes all the difference in their composure.

As a former military wife, I know first hand that early on in military training, no matter what branch of service you choose, one of the primary lessons learned is that you have no identity. In other words, you are no longer an individual. Everyone receives the same haircut, same outfit, same boots, same weapon. You wake up at the same time, and you go to bed at the same time. You are a part of one vision and you have only one focus. A young warrior in the making will learn the meaning of team work, comradery, and success as a unit, not as an island. They are taught how to face fear, and how to redirect that same fear, and sometimes anger towards defeating their enemy. He or she is taught very early on to know their weapon so well that it can be assembled in a matter of minutes. The skill level is even heightened to the point that this same task can be performed with precision even if the warrior is blindfolded. Funny how most so called Christians don't have any idea how to use the most powerful weapon given to us, the Word of God. Then we wonder why we feel so helpless against our enemy. Attention to detail is required at a much higher level by the Drill Instructor, and excuses are non-existent. And what of his or her appearance? Their clothing, shoes, and even ribbons, and medals must be meticulous both in appearance and placement.

As the young warrior learns to march to his drill instructor's cadence in the heat of the sun, and the ever nagging presence of gnats and mosquitoes, he takes away from that experience the life lesson that there is absolutely no tolerance for distractions. He learns that despite what's going on around you, your Instructor for this phase of your life must have your undivided attention, and unyielding obedience. There are early morning and late night hours devoted to marching, running, team building, leadership training, weaponry and yes, even the studying of your enemy. All in an effort to prepare you for warfare, not for civilian life. In the self same manner, all warriors in spirit should never get so comfortable that we forget the purpose for which we were born.

And what can be said for the long awaited graduation day? Yes, Graduation Day for a soldier is not just the culmination of an eight week transformation. It is his or her opportunity to say to all those in attendance, "take note that nothing I receive today came cheap. For indeed I paid for it with my blood, sweat and tears." There were countless nights spent silently wishing that you'd chosen another route to take, wishing it didn't hurt so much, and questioning whether you would ever even make it to Graduation Day. Likewise, as a warrior in spirit, you'll have these same thoughts. But you must never ever give up -- no matter how intense the notion is to do so. The impact that will emanate from what you so passionately do for the Potter and for His people will be evident all around you.

Your dedication to your call will be second to none as you remember each day that you paid dearly for that call. Your rank in the Kingdom will have been earned, not simply wished for.

CHAPTER XI
CROSSROADS

Up until very recently, it was this lump of clay's firm belief that those periods in my life in which I was confronted with a crossroad were some of the most stressful times of my forty plus years. A crossroad to me meant days on end of overwhelming feelings of fear, apprehension and indecision. It not only meant lack of sleep, a nervous queasiness in my stomach, and an overall lack of peace, but it also represented a type of uneasiness like no other. My trepidation would be laced with terrifying questions like "What if I make the wrong decision"? How can I be sure that this is God's will for me? How will this affect my children? How will this affect my career and will I look foolish to others? What will people think of my decision? These questions would seem to endlessly swirl around in my head like a big ball of confusion even during my times of prayer when I waited and begged an unseen, unheard from God for some sign of what I should do. I've heard it said that a teacher or instructor never talks during a test because all of the talking was done during their times of instruction while class was in session. At the culmination of each semester, a final exam is given which will indicate to your instructor either your ability or inability to retain what was taught in class. During this final exam or mid-term as it is sometimes referred to, you will not find the teacher explaining anything further. The time for that has passed. He or she simply issues an allotted space of time for the recall of information that they have tediously imparted into your hearing, to transition from your brain to your test paper. During test time, it will become evident to your teacher by your answers, if you weren't really paying much attention during your instruction time. Does this scenario sound familiar to any of you lumps of clay out there? I personally have spent many sleepless nights badgering the Potter with tearful pleas that sounded something like "Lord I need an answer by Tuesday…PLEASE SAY SOMETHING!!!" If your experience has been anything like mine, it has been quiet enough to hear a pin drop because your Potter/Teacher utters not a word. I've often lost patience with Him, quoting His scriptures back to Him as if **He** the writer doesn't know what **He** has said! "Didn't *you* say that if I acknowledge you in all my ways, that you would direct my paths?...HE-LLO-O, I NEED SOME DIRECTION HERE"!!!! Thank God He is so merciful even in our moments of smug, "pseudo-trust" praying. What I've discovered is that this is the time He wants you to remember to depend on the things that you were already taught in "class" and the fidelity of those things. Not in an attempt to manipulate Him into action, but in an attempt to truly use and activate the tools that you've been given to pass the test. Lessons like "All things work together for the good of them that love the Lord, and are the called according to His purpose". Or here's one, remember that day He gave homework on the subject "the steps of a good man, they are ordered by the Lord"? Or how about this one? You had a pop quiz on this one..."I'll never leave you nor forsake you, lo I am with you always, even unto the ends of the world." And you probably were napping in class, that's why you forgot about this one, "Now unto Him who is able to keep you from falling and to present you faultless before the presence of His glory with exceeding joy". No wonder David declared in Psalms that God's word is "a lamp unto my feet, and a light unto my path". When His words are in your heart, they guide you to the decisions that are right for your life. There is no big thunderous voice, or sign in the heavens, it is usually simply a small, but nagging tug at your mind and heart to go in a certain direction. I have now learned to embrace my crossroads. How can I possibly do that you ask? Simply because my crossroads are an indication to me that I am not stagnant. They serve as confirmation for me that I have been given options, choices if you will. And please understand that humans are the only specimens of creation even given the ability to choose. All other species are not blessed with options, they do nothing by choice or decision. Everything that the rest of creation does is based solely upon their nature and instinct. For example, humans are the only ones that the Potter has favored to fall in love and choose a mate, creating an emotionally charged atmosphere like lovemaking for gratification as we pro-create. Others simply breed because it is their season to. They don't know what it is to have a warm and fuzzy feeling inside when that special someone looks into your eyes, or reaches for your hand. They don't choose where they will attend school, which career path they'll take, or which house they'd like to buy. That's why instead of being so overwhelmed by the various options that have been placed before me, I've decided rather to be grateful to the Potter for honoring me enough to trust me with so many open doors. I'm not a caged bird who can only dream about flying, or sing about flying, I can fly if I just believe that I can, if I just trust Him that He's put everything in my wings necessary for me to do so. So while in the past I've lived my life worried about success or failure as opposed to just taking the journey, I now make a conscious effort to just trust God, putting one foot in front of the other, knowing that I can't just stand there at the crossroads expecting the change I desire so much for my life. I must progress in faith knowing that my God has promised never to leave me or forsake me. He has left me a Comforter whom He has promised will lead me and guide me into all truth. What truth you may wonder…it is the truth of who and what I was designed to be. We waste time staring at our crossroads, crying about our crossroads, contemplating our crossroads, and we end up missing out on some of the greatest opportunities of our lives. Without even realizing it, we say to our potential "that's okay, I won't need you because I'm too afraid to see where you can really lead me". How unfortunate for us, for you see the torment is only present as you struggle with your crossroad and your decision. You will find your place of peace once you choose a path. I've learned that the crossroad is my friend. Oh no my dear, precious lumps of clay, crossroads no longer represent a time of turmoil for me. On the contrary, they are the Potter's reminder to me that there is nothing but space and opportunity between me and my next level of progress, achievement and ultimate success. And what is ultimate success? That can only be determined by the Potter and His lump of clay. Success in my eyes may be based upon what I had planned for myself when I embarked upon that new path. Or success may be predicated upon what **God** had planned for me that I wasn't even aware of when I proceeded to walk down that chosen path. I've learned that He is with me wherever I go, and that His peace stands guard around my heart and my mind. So how can any move ever be a wrong move? Especially if it has been predicated by prayer, any move and every move can only serve as a stepping stone to my destined place in history. "The Lord is my Shepherd, I shall not want. He makes me to lie down in green pastures, He leads me beside the still waters" (that's peace); "He restores my soul" (that's strength); "He leads me in the paths of righteousness for His name's sake" (He won't steer me wrong because I've made it known that I trust Him). "Yea, though I walk through the valley of the shadow of death, I will fear no evil, for you are with me" (that's reassurance). "Thy rod and thy staff, they comfort me" (your words soothe my anxiety). "You prepare a table for me in the presence of my enemies" (you give me what I need in spite of my surroundings). "You anoint my head with oil, my cup runs over" (I feel your presence all around me). "Surely goodness and mercy shall follow me all the days of my life, (I have angels accompanying me on my journey) and I will dwell in the house of the Lord forever". (Psalms 23:1-6) My God!! I Thank you so much King Jesus! I'll never be afraid to take a step again because I have the confidence to know that you will first go before me, and that you will second, abide inside of me taking a step with me every time I take a step. Just like in the famous words of the rapper Ludicrous, "When I move, you move". Therefore all wise Potter, my eyes are fixed on your love for me, my heart trusts that you want what's best for me, and my entire life is in your hands.

CHAPTER XII
HELP THERE'S 2 OF US

HELP!!!! There's two of us, and one of us has got to go! Ladies and gentlemen in this corner, introducing the Heavyweight champion of her destiny, THE IDEAL KATRINA FOX! She is a fierce competitor, despite the strength and size of her opponent, she never disappoints, handling herself consistently as a skilled expert in her craft. Confident, tenacious, and seemingly fearless, she is a force to be reckoned with. In the opposite corner, her lifelong nemeses, THE OTHER KATRINA FOX! A force to be reckoned with in her own right, the latter is trepidatious, apprehensive, and unsure of herself, as she timidly watches the Ideal Katrina Fox in awe, wishing she could be more like her, a fearless champion every time. While no one can actually pinpoint the time in which this ongoing battle began, it is evident that these two opponents despise each other, and battle each other whenever the opportunity presents itself, which is almost on a daily basis.

Their boxing matches are intriguing to say the least, as you watch each of them display their strengths against the other's weakness. The Ideal Katrina, whose concentration seems unbreakable, is intent on showing The Other Katrina who is absolutely in charge as they enter the ring for the umpteenth time. In the beginning, the Other Katrina appears intimidated as she watches the Ideal Katrina bob and weave past disappointment, broken promises and unfulfilled dreams. Ideal Katrina's focus is evident as she mercilessly pummels The Other Katrina with that famous "Jeremiah 29:11 uppercut"! However, The Other Katrina is quick to answer back with that "you'll never be good enough left hook". They pound each other round after round, and it is difficult at times to determine who the winner is. At the end of each round, as they retreat to their corners for a word with their trainers, you can tell especially with The Ideal Katrina that there is a greater sense of urgency when she returns to the ring for the next round. Her trainer has reminded her that "No weapon formed against her is able to prosper". He has reminded her that she "can do all things through Christ who strengthens her". He has wiped the tears from her eyes and reminds her that she is favored to win. So she is swift and calculated as she returns for yet another round, determined to remain in control of the match. The Other Katrina uses time as her ally in wearing down her relentless enemy.

Every now and then she throws a jab or two, but mostly she just dances around the ring as a reminder to The Ideal Katrina that she is there to wear her down. Ideal Katrina can hear her fans cheering in the background, "we see greatness in you, we believe in you, you're a warrior, you're our hero, remember who you are!"

And deep within her heart, past all the fear that The Other Katrina attempts to impose, The Ideal Katrina knows that those words, words that she can only hear faintly sometimes above the dizzying effects of some of the blows, are absolutely the truth. Beyond all the fancy footwork that The Other Katrina displays, with her jabs of doubt, The Ideal Katrina knows that if she keeps fighting, she'll emerge the Champion once again. The Ideal Katrina knows that she is the Potter's advertisement. She is one of His favorites, for her faith in Him boasts to all who watch her life that with God all things are possible.

Do you have an Ideal Self who opposes your Real Self? Well don't be too hard on yourself, as I write these words, I am convinced that I can't be the only one who experiences this. There are days when I feel as though I can conquer the world, and then there are other days that the world seems to have my arm clinched behind my back and my collar jerked up in it's grip, sneering to me that I'd better scream UNCLE AND JUST GIVE UP! Unfortunately for the other me, I am very stubborn. I refuse to give up on what I know in my heart is possible, although my mind's eye may not always be as thoroughly convinced. As Ideal Katrina spends more time in the gym with her "trainer", her confidence, strength and stamina will increase. Her bouts with the Other Katrina will become fewer in number until they are almost non-existent. Inevitably, The Other Katrina will make her presence known very sparingly, as she will begin to finally realize that she is no match for The Ideal Katrina.

The you that you desire to be is within you, not outside of you. There is no magic relationship, job, opportunity, or other external variable that will suddenly turn you into the person that you've always wanted to be. Of course there is something to be said for self development whether that comes from counseling, self-help books, seminars, or good, honest and open friendships. But none of these resources can be substituted for time spent with the Potter, discovering not only who you are, but who He has empowered you to be because of His word. Sometimes you will have to remind yourself over and over again of what you are capable of in Him. But that's okay, just don't give up on your Ideal Self. He or she is there, possibly tired, discouraged and momentarily out of gas, but you can pick Ideal up, dust Ideal off, re-fuel Ideal and remind Ideal that losing is not an option.

The Ideal Katrina is a strong believer in God's promises. She takes them literally and because of them sees the impossible. She wants to win the world, bandage every person's wounds, and love every person's hurt away. She takes her assignment on earth and to people's lives very seriously, and doesn't lament over what her next move should be, or what her last move should have been. Her Potter is her guide, and her only desire in life is to follow Him closely so that she doesn't hinder His purpose for her moment in time. However, the Other Katrina is not as strong a believer, and looks at what is currently obvious in her real life as opposed to what God has promised. She magnifies her inadequacies and believes that her weaknesses far outweigh her strengths. The Other Katrina can see the potential in those around her, but can rarely see her own. The Other Katrina's mindset is not an asset, but rather a detriment not only to purpose but also to destiny, as the root of her existence is fear. And we all know that fear paralyzes you, keeps you from moving forward, from getting on with it.

If I haven't admonished you about anything else that has hit close to home with you in this book, please take heed to this. It is imperative that we GET ON WITH IT!!! The old cliché quite clearly informs us that "time waits for no one". I'm not sure if we really believe that to be true though. We kind of "mosey" along, sit by idly, watching life like a spectator, instead of grabbing a hold of it and participating. It's much easier to stay in our comfort zones, allowing fear to hold us hostage, as if time will continue to give us chance after chance. Even Jesus understood redeeming the time and encouraged us to work while it is day, because the night comes and then no one can work. There will be a time when the curtain will close on our scene. Our own personal night time will be here, and then our contribution to this world, our families, our churches, our communities, and even our own destinies will no longer be possible. Should you feel compelled to follow your Ideal Self in fulfilling every aspiration, accompanied with the urgency and disdain for anything stagnant, this will prove to be your life's greatest joy. Don't allow your Other Self's need for the comfortable, manageable choices that don't appear to be too overwhelming, to cheat you out of your Ideal Life. Jesus has promised that He came to give you life and that more abundantly. So what are you waiting for? Stop talking yourself out of the joys in life that by right belong to you, and go get what Jesus died to give you!

CHAPTER XIII
YOU PLAY TOO MUCH

Have you ever been playing with your friend when you were younger and suddenly one of you didn't feel like playing anymore so you got serious, but the other person didn't know that so they continued playing? Then suddenly the one who's mood had changed would blurt out, "STOP, YOU PLAY TOO MUCH!!!!" It was an unexpected turn of events, and most of the time the other person didn't even know what it was that changed your mood from giddy to solemn. Nonetheless, it brought you to the reality that fun time was over, at least for the moment, and that it was time to do something different. I think that each one of us has to come to a point in our journey where we realize that we've been playing too much. Too much playing for such a serious moment in history.

It's hard to believe that I originally wrote this chapter almost four years ago as part of my journal. As we approach the inauguration of a new President and Administration, I am reviewing the notes that I penned in 2005 and realize that some four years later, they are quite pertinent and relevant to the election process that just ended. In a political campaign there is a nomination rendered, and the nominee then accepts the candidacy. Hence a race begins, a race that involves mud slinging and debate over whether the candidate really is the person whom they've portrayed themselves to be in public. Some drop out of the race during the campaign simply due to the fact that they are unable to sustain the heat in the kitchen so to speak. But for those who are willing to tough it out, in spite of all the accusations, negative commercial ads and innuendoes, there comes an election day. A day when all the evidence is submitted, both the circumstantial evidence and the substantial, and the constituents make their choice.

It sort of reminds me of our adversary the devil. The accuser of the brethren the bible calls him. He who is constantly in the face of our Potter, attempting to persuade Him of how we are no good, and unworthy of His love and mercy. He who is persistent in his quest to convince us that we will never reach our goal of victory. He has forgotten that we have Jesus, the advocate who constantly makes us His choice in spite of all the evidence presented against us.
I, like Paul, endeavor to press towards the mark for the prize of my high call. Although aware of the smut

campaign waged against me by my enemy, the spirit that is within me reminds me to keep pressing as I will never be completely fulfilled until I am doing what I've been set apart in this world to do. Paul said he needed to apprehend that which had apprehended him. I understand him now as in my own life, it feels as though my future has come and "tagged" me "It" just like in the childhood game, leaving me in a type of discontent until I am able to take hold of what touched me. It's as if my future is saying to me every day, come and get me. This is why I thank God for His anointing, for it His anointing that has kept me from wasting time and energy trying to accomplish that for which I was not intended. I have learned that there is a difference between the anointing, that additional presence of God leading you and your ego leading you. The latter is self indulging, promotes an individual agenda, and doesn't take into account another man's sacrifice for what he or she may love doing. I've observed people in the church and the world, belittling another person's work, struggles and attempts. Claiming to be smarter, better, faster or more effective than the next person. As a result of these ideologies, we never stay in our own lane, thereby sadly neglecting what the Potter has called **us** to do. There is a gap and lack in our area of ministry because we are so busy trying to show up our fellow man by doing their job instead of the one that we have been assigned to do. The day that we are living in should insight us to be about our Father's business and not our neighbor's business. We should strive to do the work of Him that sent us as Jesus did, while it is day for the night comes when no man can work the bible admonishes us. And what is the work of Him that sent us? It is not simply singing on choirs, ushering doors, and holding annual church anniversaries and lifeless revivals. Our churches have become so filled with pomp and circumstance, matching outfits, shoes and purses, preachers "zoomin" parishioners, and parishioners zoomin preachers, that there is no room for real love, the love that Jesus spoke of. The love for a parched, and dying soul. No, no we're much too in love with and full of ourselves to concentrate on something as insignificant as another person's soul. I want people to come into my presence and find the calm for their storm that they've been longing for. People who feel alone and destitute need a haven of hope. I want to be that for them, so that I can point them to the resting place that my soul found when it was lost and searching for answers.

While originally writing this particular portion of my memoirs, I suddenly found myself unemployed, and forced to walk down a road that I'd never trod before. No job, not qualified to receive an unemployment check, and consequently no source of monthly income other than a $300 child support check. I had a home, car, one child at home, while one was in college, along with other bills to maintain and no way in which to do so. So do you think at that point in my life I cared about whether my purse and shoes matched my outfit when I went to the house of God? I needed a move from God, not just another church service. I often wondered, does anybody else feel like they're starving or is it just me? I felt something inside of me reaching out, yes craving for more, but my faithful attendance to church wasn't satisfying my appetite. I needed daily transformation and didn't want to spend another moment in a church service shouting, stomping, dancing and running while demanding my new home, car, wealth and husband. I'd grown beyond that kind of emotionalism, and just simply wanted to experience heart wrenching worship, unrestricted praise, cheeks soaked with tears, and even the freedom to lay prostrate in reverence to my Savior's magnificence. I wanted a Word that would my prick my heart and provoke my spirit to purposed sanctification. The kind of word that sends people rushing to the altars crying out "what must I do to be saved?"

Thank God, I finally found that place one day, and now any church gathering that doesn't include any and perhaps all of these experiences is not the place for me. My next level in God has to be intense and my spirit man hungers for all of these components just as my natural body hungers for food, water, and sleep.

I've personally witnessed how easy it is to get stuck being obligated to church as usual. Knowing exactly what will come next at each and every service, pretending that we don't see the obvious handwriting on the wall. The same handwriting that the Children of Israel saw when the glory of the Lord had departed from their religious gatherings. Surely "Ichabod" had been etched into the framework of our doorposts, but we continued on with business as usual, pretending not to see it. I know now that the anointing is not just for preaching or singing. The anointing is the presence of the Holy Spirit, a holy type of ease. Therefore, I need the anointing not to hit the high note when I sing, or to make everyone stand and whoop with exuberance when I preach my sermon. But rather I need it to raise my children properly, and to pay my bills on time. I need the anointing in order to stay faithfully married when problems arise and to turn the other cheek when my enemy slaps me mercilessly. Whether I'm being slapped figuratively or literally. The anointing brings fulfillment in that it empowers me for what I was set aside to do, and teaches me how not to labor in things for which I was not created. Christ's anointing has already witnessed my failures, yet endeavors to guide me through them if only I will follow its leading. Please stop playing around my fellow lumps of clay! Don't allow the progression of your life's journey, and ascension to your next level to be sacrificed as a result of your comfortable, playful present state of mind.

CHAPTER XIV
IF IT WAS A GIFT DON'T THROW IT AWAY

It is more evident to me now than ever before, that we don't really understand the power that the Potter has given us to influence our own outcome. You see, we must take the seed that God has given to us and create something that God has promised to us. Too many of us have come to hate and despise our journey, not realizing the journey is only the catalyst that God uses to enable your character to catch up with the call that has been placed upon your life. If you will make a commitment to your own destiny, even the way that people look at you will be different. Oftentimes we want people to commit themselves to us or to our various causes at different levels, yet remain uncommitted to our own sense of purpose. I am a firm believer that you can't even have more until you become more. But sometimes we are so proud of what we already do know, that we don't become nearly as enthusiastic as we should about figuring out what we **_don't_** know. If you're going to grow, you have to recognize that a temporary surrender of your present security is inevitable. There will be pain and uncertainty for sure, but these are invaluable tradeoffs for stagnation and lack of progress.

Today I learned a very valuable lesson about life. You see, I have a beautiful necklace given to me as a gift by a very dear friend of mine. I love this necklace not only because it is pretty, but because someone that means so much to me had given it to me. I hadn't been able to wear the necklace for several months now because it had gotten tangled up into all these little knots while inside my jewelry box. Day after day I would look at the necklace as I went about the task of accessorizing my outfits for work. Sadly, I'd look at it in frustration sometimes knowing that although it would be the perfect compliment to my unfinished ensemble, I had neither the time nor the patience to attempt the arduous chore of untangling it. So there the necklace sat until one day in the wee hours of the morning, although tired, I was unable to sleep. I decided to busy myself by straightening up my dresser top which seemed more productive than just staring at the ceiling. I'd already tried reading, and even praying, but was still restless, so I got up and started cleaning. Lo and behold, there amongst the clutter on my dresser was the tangled mess of a necklace, reminding me that it still awaited my time and attention so that it could be used again for that which the giver had intended. You see, I would not put the necklace back into the jewelry box once I discovered the mess that it was in. My fear was that if I put it away, I would forget about it and never be able to enjoy the pleasure that wearing it had once brought to me. If it were out of sight then it would be out of mind, and I really didn't want that. I wanted to be able to wear it again. It's just like our lives. God has given us this gift of life, and at those times when we discover that we have somewhat made a mess of it, instead of taking the time to work through it in honor of the one who gave it to us, we just ignore what's wrong, and avoid taking the time to work the kinks out.

Of course there were other things that I could have given my attention to during this bout with insomnia, but no other task had experienced the type of procrastination that my mangled necklace had. Therefore, I decided to give it the long overdue attention that it both needed and deserved. It's so funny how your mind works sometimes. There was a part of me that wanted to give up before I even got started. That part of me was the memory of previous attempts which reminded me of how frustrating this could be, and how I had failed so many times before. At the onset I started thinking that it was useless to even try, and something told me to just throw the necklace away. I think the reason that I was able to dismiss that thought both this time, and at prior times when my attempts to detangle had failed, was that my very kind and loving sister/friend had given the necklace to me. What would I be saying about the value of her gift to me if I just simply threw it away? So I tricked myself! I told myself that this necklace was like my life, a beautiful gift that the Potter had given to me, and that I had inadvertently tangled it up into many formidable little knots. But if I would slowly take the time to get to the "root" or center of every tangled knot, that eventually I would experience the joy of this gift once again. So one by one, knot by knot, I persevered. Sometimes thinking that I might have been making it worst, because just as it would look like I'd untangled one knot, it would seem like I'd created several more. And yes, just like life it got worst before it got better. But you can't imagine my sense of accomplishment and the exuberance I felt when two hours after the start of my challenge, I was looking at the finished product. My beautiful necklace was free of confusion, and right away I was pondering what outfit I could possibly wear it with the next day. Was I excited about the necklace? Of course I was, but I was more excited over my newfound knowledge that no matter how tangled, mangled, or hopeless your life may appear to be, with a little time, patience, and a few deep breaths every now and then, you can unravel every twisted, knotted up mess on the inside and outside of you. Whether your mess was caused by neglect, worsened by procrastination, or just merely a series of mishaps, there is always hope. You know, there were several times that I considered taking my necklace to a jeweler. Maybe he or she would be better skilled at something like this, but no this was MY necklace! I'd caused it to be in the condition that it was, nobody else, and it was up to me to take responsibility for fixing it. I just had to work through my frustration, and be patient. Move slowly, meticulously, pay strict attention to every move and be calculated in my progression. And guess what? I wore my necklace that Saturday night to a concert. It was the perfect compliment to my new maxi dress. I had to travel out of town and didn't want it to get tangled again in my suitcase, so I hung it up in my car around the rear view mirror. I already have another ornament that hangs there, a gift from another one of my "sistas", a beautiful embellished cross. Well at first I paid it no attention, but as I traveled down the highway on my way to Charleston, I looked over and noticed that the cross was hanging ever so perfectly in the middle of my necklace. Do you get it my fellow lumps of clay? You have to remember that as you travel along life's highway, if you keep God as the center of your life, He'll keep it untangled for you!

CHAPTER XV
<u>THE CONCLUSION OF THE MATTER</u>

My best friend (human that is) asked me the other day how my book was coming. I told him that I felt stalled, and that I didn't want to write just to be writing. I wanted to have something to say to you my readers. Something significant as I approached the end of my time with you. For if the words written on these pages didn't impact your life in some way, then I've not done what I set out to do. The lyricist Johnson Oatman Jr. (1895) wrote the song "there's not a friend like the lowly Jesus, no not one, no not one". And it has been my endeavor throughout the pages of these memoirs to introduce to you the man who has been my friend for the entirety of my life. All the episodes of it, both good and bad. He was never a seasonal or fair weather friend, but one who has seen me at my worst, and still loved me so unconditionally. For in doing so, my hope is that you too perhaps will find that your journey is not as unbearable as it has sometimes felt.

I've not lived the perfect life, and I've made plenty of mistakes…still making them. But, this friend of mine, this Potter who specializes in love and creativity, has been relentless in His pursuit of me, just as I believe He has been for you. I beg of you to give Him all of you! The uncertainty, the brokenness, the lack of confidence, and even the shattered dreams, give it all to Him. He knows how to put you back together, and He knows how to cause it all to make sense. He is the glue that your life so desperately needs.

After explaining to this friend my vision for the book, he called it a "Living Book". I'd never thought of it in those terms, but my eyes began to fill up with tears at the concept of that. It was indeed a book for living in that not only was it being added to as I walked out my journey, but it was hopefully going to assist others with living their lives more triumphantly.

As a teenager growing up in the holiness church, there was a song that would touch my heart whenever I heard it. Although I was young, I even remember how it sounded when it was sang at my Great Grandfather Mose Spencer's funeral. "If I can help somebody as I pass along; If I can cheer somebody with a word or song; If I can show somebody that he's travelin' wrong, then my living shall not be in vain, then my living shall not be in vain. If I can do my duty as a good man ought; If I can bring back beauty to a world up wrought; If I can spread love's message as the Master taught, then my living shall not be in vain".

Therefore my fellow lumps of clay, it is with a heart full of gratitude that I say to you, may the ups and downs of my life's journey chronicled for you in these memoirs, prove to be the boost you need, and the reminder you crave that the Potter really does have it all under control. You may not, but He **always** does. He is ultimately the peace that you seek, the fulfillment that you desire, and the joy that you're starving for. He is the author, executive producer, and director of this ugly, yet simultaneously beautiful thing we call life. So it is because of Him and in spite of me, the part of me that always tries to get in the way, that I bid you both Grace and peace my fellow lumps of clay….Grace for your journey and peace for your hearts and minds as you experience your moments in time on the Potter's Wheel.

SCRIPTURE REFERENCES

CHAPTER I

4   "Whatever your hands find to do"
Colossians 3:23-24/ Eccles 9:10

CHAPTER II

10   "Every man's work shall be tried by Fire"
I Corinthians 3:13

11   "God knows our frame"
Psalms 103:14

12   "He is despised and rejected of men"
Isaiah 53:3

13   "When my heart is overwhelmed, lead me to the rock"
Psalms 31:2

CHAPTER III

21   "Who for the joy that was set before him endured the cross and despised the shame"
Hebrews 12:2

27   "Greater love hath no man than this that he lay down his life…"
John 15:13

CHAPTER IV

34   "A man's gift maketh room for him…"
Proverbs 18:16

35   "Blessed be the Lord my strength which teacheth my hands to war and my fingers to fight"
Psalms 144:1

36 "...No good thing will he withhold from them that walk uprightly"
Psalms 84:11b

CHAPTER V
38 "Hope deferred maketh the heart sick"
Proverbs 13:12

39 "...But I follow after that I may apprehend that for which also I am apprehended of Christ Jesus"
Phillipians 3:12

44 "And ye shall seek me and find me when you shall search for me with all your heart"
Jeremiah 29:13

46 "For we have not an high priest which cannot be touched with the feelings of our infirmities...."
Hebrews 4:15

47 "Come unto me all ye that labor and are heavy laden and I will give you rest"
Matthew 11:28

48 "And he saith unto them follow me and I will make you fishers of men"
Matthew 4:19

CHAPTER VI
55 "He goeth before them and the sheep follow him for they know his voice and a stranger they will not follow'
John 10:4b-5a

CHAPTER VIII

65	"Out of the abundance of the heart, the mouth speaketh" Matthew 12:34b

CHAPTER X

84	"I returned and saw under the sun that the race is not to the swift nor the battle to the strong" Ecclesiastes 9:11a
	"But he that endureth to the end shall be saved" Matthew 10:22b
	"For the weapons of our warfare are not carnal…" II Corinthians 10:4
85	"Thou therefore endure hardness as a good soldier of Jesus Christ" II Timothy 2:3-4

CHAPTER XI

89	"And we know that all things work together for the good of them…" Romans 8:28
	"The steps of a good man are ordered by the Lord" Psalms 31:23a
	"Now unto him that is able to present you faultless before the presence…" Jude 24
	"Thy word is a lamp unto my feet, and a light unto my path". Psalms 119:105

CHAPTER XII

94   "For I know the thoughts that I think towards you saith the Lord…."
Jeremiah 29:11

"No weapon that is formed against you shall prosper…"
Isaiah 54:17

"I can do all things through Christ which strengthens me"
Phillipians 4:13

SONG REFERENCES

"The Potter's House"
Walter Hawkins (1990)

"I Believe I Can Fly"
 R. Kelly (1996)

"Stand Up"
Ludicrous & Kanye West (1993)

"There's Not A Friend"
Johnson Oatman Jr. (1895)

"My Living Shall Not Be In Vain"
Alma Bazel Androzzo (1945)

ACKNOWLEDGEMENTS

I am eternally grateful as I believe that the strength and integrity of my Christian walk today is attributed to the foundational truths instilled in me as a child by Reverends Samuel and Elvina Manigault. Thank you to my parents Rutley and Juanita Fox, and my siblings Yvette, Rutley, and Lillie for the love, prayers and validation that you gave to me early in life, up until this very moment. Poppy, Shannon & CJ for being the wind beneath my wings....I will always love and adore you. Bishop Sammy C. Smith, for being my life coach for 12 years as the Potter had His way with me. Apostle Ron Carpenter Jr., for the restoration of my faith in ministry and the resuscitation of my dreams. The words spoken from your mouth were the lifeline that rescued my bruised and wounded spirit from drowning in a sea of church disillusionment. To my sisters in Christ who have laughed with me, cried with me, and danced with me on this crazy Potter's Wheel. To my Editor, Tita Johnson who at times seemed more passionate about this project than I was, I am forever indebted to you for your tireless efforts, encouragement and faith in me. You all have encouraged me in your own unique way, reminding me that it is imperative for each of us to do what we were placed on this planet to do, so that we may operate in the vocation that we have been summons to by God. Thank you for your indelible imprint upon my heart, and upon my life!

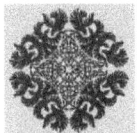

www.ingramcontent.com/pod-product-compliance
Lightning Source LLC
Chambersburg PA
CBHW051805040426
42446CB00007B/525